WITHDRAWN

DE PROPRIETATIBUS LITTERARUM

edenda curat

C. H. VAN SCHOONEVELD

Indiana University

Series Maior, 9

THE BODY POLITIC

A Political Metaphor in Renaissance English Literature

by

DAVID GEORGE HALE

State University of New York,
Brockport

1971

MOUTON

THE HAGUE · PARIS

LIBRARY OF CONGRESS CATALOG CARD NUMBER: 77-165143

Printed in The Netherlands by Mouton & Co., Printers, The Hague.

ACKNOWLEDGMENTS

My major debt is to Professor John L. Lievsay who supervised the present work as a doctoral dissertation at Duke University. Professors S. K. Heninger Jr., Arthur B. Ferguson, and Holger O. Nygard also provided substantial advice and counsel. Earlier studies in literature and politics, incorporated here, were written under the guidance of J. A. Bryant Jr., Theodore H. Banks, and Alexander Cowie. More recently I have received assistance from Katherine A. Pantzer, D. J. Barr, and William R. Erwin. For making my task easier I am grateful to the staffs of the libraries of Duke University, the University of North Carolina, the University of Cincinnati, Harvard University, and Princeton University. Many other libraries have made their resources available on microfilm or through interlibrary loan.

In my quotations from primary sources I have partially modernized the orthography (i-j, u-v, etc.) and occasionally regularized the punctuation.

Portions of my material, in different form, have appeared in *Neuphilologische Mitteilungen, Comparative Literature Studies,* and *Shakespeare Quarterly*; the editors of these journals have kindly given me permission to reprint.

My wife, Margaret, has sustained me through many tribulations.

D. G. H.

PREFACE

The analogy between society and the human body is used with more frequency, variety, and seriousness than any of the correspondences which compose the 'Elizabethan world picture'. The comparison is employed to defend and attack the established church, to promote order and obedience to secular rulers, and to criticize political and economic abuses. The purpose of this book is to trace the history of the analogy from classical antiquity, to examine its flourishing in Elizabethan literature, and to account for its loss of validity in the early seventeenth century.

The bodies politic and natural have similar form and possess a similar life or mind. There are two traditions in the history of the analogy. The first considers the balance of elements or humors in a body; analyses of the diseases of the state derive from this concept. The second describes the parts of a body, their structure and interrelation. The fable of the belly and the rebellious members is one aspect of this tradition. Both traditions appear in the Greek writers who discuss the unity and well-being of the *polis*. During the Middle Ages the Pauline doctrine of the Church as the mystical body of Christ was the source of many of the elaborate applications of organic analogies in political and religious writings in prose and verse.

In the Renaissance the metaphor of the body politic was affected by the rise of national states, the Reformation, and the revival of Platonism. Henry VIII's assumption of the headship of the Church of England raised profound questions about the nature of the bodies to which men belonged; More's *Dialogue Concerning Tyndale* and Gardiner's *Oration of True Obedience* exemplify two sides of the controversy. The dissolution of the monasteries and other factors produced economic distress, diseases of the realm which are analyzed in Starkey's *Dialogue* and other works.

During the reign of Elizabeth the analogy continued to find a wide

range of applications. The horrors of unnatural rebellion were denounced; Martin Marprelate and his opponents debated the place of
the bishops in the body of the Church; poets and playwrights, especially
Dekker and Shakespeare, found both comic and serious possibilities in
the comparison. Dekker's *The Dead Terme*, Tomkis' *Lingua*, Forset's
Comparative Discourse, and Shakespeare's *Coriolanus* are dominated
by the metaphor. The imagery of the body permeates Shakespeare's
play, yet the action questions the applicability of organic analogies to
political situations.

In the seventeenth century the analogy was still used – by Bacon,
Burton, Donne, Laud, and others – while its validity was effectively
challenged on several grounds. A materialistic view of nature (*e.g.*
Bacon and Hobbes) replaced the old hylozoistic one which had given a
scientific basis to the analogy. More immediate was the adoption of
covenant theology and the idea of a social contract by the Calvinists.
If society is contractually rather than naturally or divinely established,
it is easier to effect a thorough reformation and to take action against
an unsatisfactory ruler. The transition is found in Milton's prose works.
His early pamphlets attack the bishops as diseased members; his defence of regicide rejects the organic analogy and relies on the contractual origin of the state. For quite different purposes Hobbes also
makes much of a contract which produces the Leviathan, an artificial,
machine-like man.

Since the Restoration the phrase 'body politic' has been simply a
synonym for 'the state', although there was a revival of interest in
organic analogies in the nineteenth century, *e.g.* Carlyle and Herbert
Spencer.

CONTENTS

I

INTRODUCTION

On November 11, 1620, the good ship *Mayflower* rode at anchor in the dark waters off the coast of Massachusetts. On that day forty-one men affixed their signatures to a document which in part says: "We ... Having undertaken for the Glory of God and advancement of the Christian Faith and Honour of our King and Countrey, a Voyage to plant the first Colony in the Northern Parts of Virginia, do by these presents solemnly and mutually, in the presence of God and one of another, covenant and combine ourselves together into a Civil Body Politike, for our better ordering and preservation. . . ."[1] These were Englishmen, come from Nottinghamshire by way of Leyden, seeking to establish themselves and their families in a place where they could worship God in what their countrymen regarded as their very peculiar way.

A dozen years before, the year in which this little congregation left Scrooby, the audience at the Globe Theater beside the Thames had listened to "a humorous patrician and one that loves the cup of hot wine with not a drop of allaying Tiber in 't", Menenius Agrippa, quiet a company of rebellious plebeians by telling them "a pretty tale":

> *Men.*   There was a time when all the body's members
> Rebell'd against the belly. . . .
> The senators of Rome are this good belly,
> And you the mutinous members; for examine
> Their counsels and their cares, digest things rightly
> Touching the weal o' th' common, you shall find
> No public benefit which you receive
> But it proceeds or comes from them to you
> And no way from yourselves.[2]

[1]   William Bradford, *Of Plymouth Plantation: 1620-1647*, ed. Samuel E. Morison (New York, 1952), pp. 75-76.
[2]   William Shakespeare, *Coriolanus*, II.i.51-53; I.i.99-100, 152-158, in: *The Complete Plays and Poems of William Shakespeare*, ed. William A. Neilson and Charles J. Hill (Cambridge, Mass., 1942).

It is improbable that any of Pastor Robinson's company heard, or even heard about, *Coriolanus*. But the phrase 'Body Politike' and Menenius' application of his fable both express a comparison between a human body and a human society – specifically Plymouth Plantation and republican Rome. There are, however, significant differences between the passages just quoted. The Pilgrim Fathers are, by an act of conscious will, covenanting and combining to bring a new religious, social, and political entity into being. This entity, in addition to being a semi-autonomous political unit, also possesses a corporate personality recognized by the common law. Shakespeare's Menenius is attempting to end a mutiny by appealing to a shared understanding of the necessary hierarchy of rank and authority within Rome and the functional interrelationship of the body's members. Menenius' comparison is more than a device of rhetoric; it is a statement of a truth, of a correspondence between microcosm and macrocosm which reveals an identical condition in both. In contrast to the Mayflower Compact, *Coriolanus* contains what we may call a living metaphor; the organic imagery is substantial both in quantity and in the conceptual support it gives to the play. This difference is a significant aspect of the great historical process called the Renaissance.

The task of this book is to study the metaphor of the body politic in England during the Renaissance – a period which can be defined as extending from Henry VIII's break with Rome, the figurative dismembering of the universal *corpus ecclesias*, to the death of Charles I, the literal decapitation of the English *corpus politicum*. Although such a division of the flow of history is arbitrary, these two events provide convenient foci for discussing certain aspects of the idea of the body politic. The history of the metaphor is, perhaps, a guide to certain aspects of the Western intellectual heritage. The comparison between society or the state and a human body retained its vitality because for a long time certain assumptions about man and the nature of the universe in which he lived were accepted without significant or effective challenge. When these assumptions – political, religious, scientific, economic – were challenged by the pressure of events and by other assumptions, then the living metaphor of the body politic became a dead phrase which is simply synonymous with 'the state', having no further meanings implied or accepted.

In his introductory discussion of English literature in the early seventeenth century Douglas Bush lists a series of questions which troubled the men of that time, among them: "Is society an organism actuated by religious motives or an aggregate of individuals actuated by economic self-interest?"[3] The answer to this question has been reduced to handbook simplicity: "The old analogy for the body politic had been the human body, a living organism. The new analogy, insisted upon by Locke, was a business contract. . . . Society, in fact, was no longer conceived as an organism, but as a joint stock company."[4] This transition from "organism" to "joint stock company" is a specific and significant example of what is meant when the Renaissance is defined as the transition from medieval to modern.

Though they may be oversimplified, statements in handbooks are usually based on the substantial efforts of many scholars; the reasons are not always clear why such statements need more belaboring. Although many writers have discussed, usually briefly, aspects of the idea of the body politic, no one has devoted an extended work to bringing these aspects together. The best introduction to the subject is E. M. W. Tillyard's *The Elizabethan World Picture*.[5] He treats the body politic through quotations from Shakespeare, Thomas Starkey, Nicholas Breton, and I.K.'s translation of Romei's *Courtier's Academy*, and says that the comparison is "a commonplace" whose "usual intention is to establish the unity and mutually necessary ranks of the body politic...".[6] But Tillyard's small volume has such a broad scope that there is no detailed nor penetrating discussion of any of the many topics he mentions.

As is clear from Tillyard's book, the idea of the body politic is part of a large complex of relationships between microcosms and macrocosm.[7] These 'little worlds' exhibit the same structure of composition as

[3] Douglas Bush, *English Literature in the Earlier Seventeenth Century: 1600-1660*, 2nd ed. (Oxford, 1962), p. 2.
[4] Vivian de S. Pinto, *The English Renaissance: 1510-1688*, 2nd ed. (New York, 1950), p. 95.
[5] E. M. W. Tillyard, *The Elizabethan World Picture* (New York, 1944); pp. 94-99. See also James E. Phillips, *The State in Shakespeare's Greek and Roman Plays*, Columbia University Studies in English and Comparative Literature No. 149 (New York, 1940), pp. 61-112; Theodore Spencer, *Shakespeare and the Nature of Man*, 2nd ed. (Cambridge, Mass., 1949), pp. 1-20; and Ernest W. Talbert, *The Problem of Order: Elizabethan Political Commonplaces and an Example of Shakespeare's Art* (Chapel Hill, N.C., 1962). These books are concerned with the body politic as an expression of political order and authority which becomes royal absolutism.
[6] Tillyard, *The Elizabethan World Picture*, p. 95.
[7] See George P. Conger, *Theories of Macrocosms and Microcosms in the History of Philosophy* (New York, 1922); Rudolph Allers, "Microcosmus: From Anaximandros to Paracelsus", *Traditio*, II (1944), 319-407; and C. A. Patrides,

the 'great world'. These similarities permit some writers to argue from one 'world' to another; in some cases the correspondences extend to a relationship of cause and effect. And, as in the case of the body politic, a microcosm is simultaneously a component part of the macrocosm. The inversion of the idea of the body politic, describing the individual in terms of the state, is found in such works as Phineas Fletcher's *The Purple Island* (1633) and in banter of one of Dekker's characters:

> *Spungius.* All the members of my bodie are in rebellion one against another. . . . But in this rebellion, what uproars do they make, my belly cries to my mouth, who dost not gape and feed me. . . . But then my feet like lazie rogues lie still, and had rather do nothing, then run to and fro, to purchase any thing.⁸

Another set of correspondences is geographical; one Greek writer compared the Peloponnesus to a man's head, the Isthmus of Corinth to the neck, Pagae and Megara to the shoulders, and so on.⁹ The inversion of this correspondence provides the imagery for Lord Herbert of Cherbury's "A Description", Donne's "Elegie XVIII: Loves Progress", and a delightful passage in *The Comedy of Errors* (III.ii.116-43) about the countries to be found in a globe-like kitchen wench. Finally there is the comparison of the human body to the universe, which is fundamental to astrology. Widespread in medieval and renaissance literature, such comparisons also produced an artistic tradition which is merrily ridiculed in Dekker's *The Raven's Almanacke* (1609).¹⁰

The point which Tillyard does not make is that of all these various relationships the comparison between the human body and society is one of the most frequent, is used with greater ingenuity for a wider variety of purposes, and is a vehicle for the expression of religious and political ideas of the deepest significance. All too frequently a modern commentator will dismiss an Elizabethan analysis of the parts of a body politic as an "inevitable medieval commonplace" or with some equally disparaging remark. But the recurring application of organic analogies

---

"The Microcosm of Man", *Notes and Queries*, CCV (1960), 54-56, and CCVIII (1963), 282-86.

⁸ Thomas Dekker and Philip Massinger, *The Virgin Martyr* (III.iii.45-46, 50-51, 59-60) in: *The Dramatic Works of Thomas Dekker*, ed. Fredson Bowers, 5 vols. (Cambridge, 1953), III, 425-26. See also Sir John Davies of Hereford, *Mirum in Modum* (1602).

⁹ Strabo, cited in Robert Burton, *The Anatomy of Melancholy*, ed. A. R. Shilleto, 3 vols. (London, 1896), I, 38-39.

¹⁰ For the iconography see Fritz Saxl, "Macrocosm and Microcosm in Medieval Pictures", in: *Lectures*, 2 vols. (London, 1957), I, 58-72.

is not necessarily routine, or commonplace, or thoughtlessly stereo-typed. The comparison has been used to buttress arguments for and against many kinds of social, political, and religious institutions – the Athenian *polis*, the Hellenistic world-empire, the medieval papacy, Tudor England, and the humble congregation aboard the *Mayflower*. Men of science from Aristotle through Sir Willam Harvey have testified to the validity of the analogy. It has been used in almost every literary genre – drama, poem, essay, sermon, philosophic treatise and political pamphlet. Sophocles, Cicero, St. Thomas Aquinas, John Milton, and a veritable host of other writers, well known and anonymous, have made significant use of the idea of the body politic.

There are two kinds of organic analogies which have been used politically, though the types are sometimes mixed in practice. The first considers the bodies natural and politic to be composed of parts which are in certain structural and functional relationships to each other. The fable of the belly and the rebellious members, whether attributed to Aesop or Menenius, is one aspect of this tradition. Another aspect is the hierarchical description of the parts – head, arms, hands, heart, legs, feet, and so on. In medieval literature the three-fold division of man-kind into nobility, clergy, and commons is sometimes presented in these terms.[11] There are also many cases in which the analogy is simplified into a differentiation between a head which rules and a body which obeys.

The second kind of organic analogy considers man as composed of the four humors, which correspond to the four elements of earth, water, air, and fire. According to a tradition which goes back at least to Empedocles, elemental man contains the humors in a proper balance and proportion; imbalance causes disease. Although the humors are rarely equated with social classes, writers from Plato through Robert Burton have discussed the sicknesses of the body politic, and usually have some specific cures to suggest.

The idea of the body politic is closely related to two other ideas current in the Renaissance. The first is the legal fiction of the Elizabethan lawyers that the sovereign possesses two bodies – one na-

[11] See Ruth Mohl, *The Three Estates in Medieval and Renaissance Literature*, Columbia University Studies in English and Comparative Literature No. 114 (New York, 1935). This work is an exhaustive collection and description of pas-sages primarily from French and English literature. Although not chiefly con-cerned with the idea of the body politic, Miss Mohl does provide some helpful comments, especially about the disappearance of the literature of estates during the sixteenth century.

tural and mortal, the other mystical and immortal.[12] The king is immortal insofar as he holds an immortal office as head of a *corpus mysticum et politicum*. This dual nature of the king as both microcosm and part of the macrocosm receives its finest literary expression in Shakespeare's *Richard II*. The second idea is that of the "Great Chain of Being". This concept rests on three basic principles: plenitude, or the fullness of creation; qualitative continuity, or the varying degrees of perfection present in the world; and unilinear gradation of this series of created forms into one complete and consistent hierarchy.[13] Acceptance of a meaningful analogy between the bodies natural and politic nearly always involves the acceptance of these principles. In both bodies there exist all possible parts, which may be ranked in one order. Rather than continuity, which emphasizes the relationship of one link in the chain to the next, the idea of a body politic stresses the unity which permeates the whole body.

The subject of this book falls between the disciplines of the history of literature and the history of ideas. The metaphor of the body politic is a means of expressing a relationship, a use of language to convey thought. This language is used with varying degrees of competence and clarity sometimes becoming poetry through an artistic elevation and intensification. These chapters will collect substantial and representative examples of discussion of the body politic and will analyze in detail some important works to show the specific meanings which the analogy has for their authors. The examples are chosen from a variety of literary types; in a study of this kind there is no point in restricting consideration to prose tracts, for example, or to verse. Nor should lack of purely literary merit exclude a work.

The chapter on background traces the development of the metaphor from its origins in Periclean Athens through the Middle Ages, when the analogy expressed the elaborate but intelligible order of the universe. Tillyard says that the world picture of the Elizabethans was only a "simplified version of a much more complicated medieval picture".[14]

---

[12]   See Ernst H. Kantorowicz, *The King's Two Bodies: A Study in Mediaeval Political Theology* (Princeton, 1957). This brilliant discussion contains much information of direct relevance for the study of the idea of the body politic in Renaissance England, especially its essay on *Richard II* (pp. 24-41). See also F. W. Maitland, "The Body Politic", in: *Selected Essays*, ed. H. D. Hazeltine, *et al.* (Cambridge, 1936), pp. 240-56.
[13]   Arthur O. Lovejoy, *The Great Chain of Being* (Cambridge, Mass., 1936), p. 59.
[14]   Tillyard, *The Elizabethan World Picture*, p. 4.

On the other hand, J. W. Allen suggests that "under Henry VIII and Edward VI ... the medieval conceptions received ... a fresh expression".[15] Fritz Caspari's chapter on Thomas Starkey carries this suggestion further: "The idea of an 'organic society', though outwardly similar to the medieval conception, received a new context and significance as a result of the humanists' return to the authors and values of classical antiquity, particularly to Plato."[16] The three main chapters examine the flourishing and decline of the metaphor during the Renaissance. The problems of Reformation and the subsequent economic distress are the new context of which Caspari speaks. For Shakespeare and his contemporaries the organic analogy was an effective device against all kinds of external and internal dangers. But by the time of the Civil War the new science and a new analogy, that of the social contract, provided men with a quite different pattern of thinking and of communicating their ideas.

I have tried to minimize reference to events and writers on the Continent, but this is a difficult task because of the extreme importance of writers like Calvin and Bodin and of events like the Massacre of St. Bartholomew's Day. Because conflicts between rulers and minority religious groups developed earlier in France and Germany than in England, the conduct of the struggle between Puritan and King in England was considerably influenced by what had happened and what had been written across the Channel. In discussing the literary expression of political thought in the sixteenth and seventeenth centuries, it is well to remember one of J. W. Allen's *caveats*. Much political thinking is not so much rational thought as it is an attempt to justify one's actions, to adjust ideas to circumstances.[17] We ought, therefore, to be constantly aware of events as well as the progression of ideas as revealed in literary texts.

[15] J. W. Allen, *A History of Political Thought in the Sixteenth Century* (London, 1928), p. 134.
[16] Fritz Caspari, *Humanism and the Social Order in Tudor England* (Chicago, 1954), p. 114.
[17] Allen, *Political Thought in the Sixteenth Century*, p. xvii.

II

BACKGROUND: CLASSICAL AND MEDIEVAL

The 'pretty tale' told by Shakespeare's Menenius is but one example of the idea of a body politic in Renaissance English literature; behind the fable is a long and moderately complicated tradition whose story must first be traced. The task of this chapter is threefold: to outline the development of the various kinds of analogies between man and the state, to consider the concepts which underlie these analogies, and to demonstrate the variety of applications given these analogies. It seems best to arrange the material chronologically. The first half of the chapter deals with the beginnings of the idea of a body politic in the Greek, Hellenistic, and early Christian periods; the second half treats the more extensive use of organic analogies in the Middle Ages and shows how the practice of some sixteenth-century writers is anticipated in the fifteenth. This chapter necessarily covers much that is not specifically English because medieval civilization, if anything, was international. Shakespeare's plays were acted in a theater beside the Thames River; but the story of the metaphor of the body politic begins many centuries earlier in a city near the warm waters of the Aegean Sea.

CLASSICAL

The origins of the idea of a body politic are to be found in ancient Greece, especially in the age of Pericles when the Athenian *polis* achieved an extraordinary amount of political unity and developed, appropriately, the organic analogy to express this unity.[1] The Athenian

[1] See Wilhelm Nestle, "Die Fabel des Menenius Agrippa", *Klio*, XXI (1927), 350-60, reprinted in his *Griechische Studien* (Stuttgart, 1944), pp. 502-16. For the *polis* I rely on H. D. F. Kitto, *The Greeks* (Harmondsworth, 1951), pp. 1-12, 64-79, 152-69 and George H. Sabine, *A History of Political Theory*, 2nd ed. (New York, 1950), pp. 1-40. Barker (Ernest Barker, *Greek Political Theory: Plato and his predecessors*, 2nd ed. [London, 1925], pp. 232-37) takes up the organic theory

citizen, although he applied himself to his own affairs, felt he could express himself most completely as a member of the *polis*; he was incomplete and unfulfilled without it. Thucydides has Pericles say in the famous funeral oration, "we alone regard the man who takes no part in public affairs, not as one who minds his own business, but as good for nothing . . .".[2] The democracy was a fragile thing; it was not really established until 594 B.C. with the Constitution of Solon, and it could not effectively survive the blows of the Peloponnesian War and the conquests of Alexander. But while the democracy flourished, it involved all of the citizens of the *polis* in public affairs to an unprecedented degree. The *polis* was large enough to be relatively self-sustaining and thereby independent; it was small enough to make widespread active citizenship possible. Debate, discussion, elections, the holding of office – all were the daily concern of all citizens, not only interest but (in varying degrees) active participation: "you will find united in the same persons an interest in private and in public affairs . . .".[3] So bound up are citizen and city that for Pericles the praise of Athens and her constitution is the highest praise for those who fall in her wars.

Our first good examples of the use of the human body as an analogy to express the unity of the state are found in writings dating from the middle of the fourth century before Christ. The idea occurs in the *Areopagiticus* (17) (355 B.C.) of Isocrates: "For the soul of a state is nothing else than its polity, having as much power over it as does the mind over the body; for it is this which deliberates upon all questions, seeking to preserve what is good and to ward off what is disastrous; and it is this which of necessity assimilates to its own nature the laws, the public orators and the private citizens; and all the members of the state must fare well or ill according to the kind of polity under which they live".[4] This passage emphasizes the participation of all citizens in the political life of the *polis* and the dependence of their welfare on the proper functioning of the constitution of the city.

The public spirit which held the *polis* together the Greeks called *homonoia*.[5] Beginning in the last third of the fifth century, as the *poleis*

---

of the state in terms which derive from the revival of the analogy in the nineteenth century by such writers as Carlyle and Herbert Spencer.

[2]   Thucydides, *History of the Peloponnesian War* (II.xl.2), trans. C. Foster Smith, Loeb Library, 4 vols. (London & New York, 1919-23), I, 319.

[3]   Thucydides, *History*, I, 329.

[4]   In *Isocrates*, trans. George Norlin and Larue Van Hook, Loeb Library, 3 vols. (London & New York, 1929-45), II, 113.

[5]   Nestle, "Die Fabel des Menenius Agrippa", p. 353.

became increasingly unable to cope with the problems of war, trade, and colonial administration on a large scale, there grew up a considerable body of literature calling for the renewal of *homonoia*. In this literature the idea of a body politic is used both as an ideal against which to measure present difficulties often by describing the present in terms of physical disease. When in the *Panathenaicus* Isocrates again says that "every polity is the soul of the state", he does so to contrast the present condition of the democracy with the happier days of the early Athenian kings whose rule was so good.[6]

The political writings of Plato are filled with an awareness of the failings of Athenian democracy. The *Republic* begins as a search for the meaning of justice. At first the analogy between the individual and the state is used as a method of inquiry: ". . . if we found some larger thing that contained justice and viewed it there, we should more easily discover its nature in the individual man."[7] In two places in the *Republic* Plato uses imagery of disease to describe a state. In Book III he traces the rise of a simple, rural state, "the healthy state" (*polis . . . ygies*). The addition of luxuries – sweetmeats, furniture, incense, and so on – produces a "fevered state" (*phlegmainousan polis*).[8] The cure for this "festering" is too often the multiplication of petty laws by those who hope to find "a panacea that will restore their health".[9] This concept lies behind a long passage in the *Crito* in which Socrates compares his concern for the welfare of the *polis* with an athlete's concern for his own health.[10]

The Athenian democracy depended on the part-time efforts of the citizens; this could, and did, lead to apathy or a kind of political dilettantism. Plato proposed a rigorous application of the principle of the division of labor: "each one man must perform one social service for which his nature was best adapted."[11] Men are not born for themselves alone, but also for their friends and their country. Plato urged the concentration of political authority in the hands of a specialized class of Guardians or Philosopher-Kings. Only in a state thus rationally directed could there be the proportion and harmony so necessary to the

---

[6] *Isocrates*, II, 459.
[7] Plato, *The Republic* (434 D), trans. Paul Shorey, Loeb Library, 2 vols. (London & New York, 1930), I, 367.
[8] Plato, *Republic* (372 E), I, 161.
[9] Plato, *Republic* (425 E-426 D), I, 339-43.
[10] Plato, *Crito* (47 B-48 B), trans. Harold N. Fowler, Loeb Library (London & New York, 1928), pp. 163-67.
[11] Plato, *Republic* (433 A), I, 367.

health of the state. In a sense this is a perfection of the organic theory in that each member of society is given a function to perform and he most completely expresses his nature through the performance of this function; an interest in something else (usually politics) detracts from an individual's participation in the body politic. On the other hand, such rigid specialization may have the effect of destroying the spirit of *homonoia* which binds men together.

In the *Laws*, his last important political writing, Plato shifts his interest from a faith in the wisdom of the Philosopher-Kings of the *Republic* to the law as a "golden chain" to hold the state together. In a sense this is a substitution for *homonoia*. But we still find Plato using the organic analogy to portray a peaceful state: "The highest good, however, is neither war nor civil strife . . . but peace with one another and friendly feeling. . . . For imagine a man supposing that a human body was best off when it was sick and purged with physic, while never giving a thought to the case of a body that needs no physic at all! Similarly, with regard to the well-being of a state . . ., that man will never make a genuine statesman who pays attention primarily to the needs of foreign warfare. . . ."[12]

The organic nature of the state is more specifically enunciated by Aristotle. Early in Book I of the *Politics* he says, ". . . it is evident that the state is a creature of nature and that man is by nature a political animal".[13] This sentence affirms two of the basic concepts in the idea of a body politic: society is natural, not a creation of man; man's highest nature is to be a part of society, not an individual. Man is, Aristotle continues, given by nature the power of speech and a sense of justice to fit him for this social role. "Thus the state is by nature clearly prior to the family and the individual, since the whole is of necessity prior to the part: for example if the whole body be destroyed, there will be no foot or hand. . . . The proof that the state is a creature of nature and prior to the individual is that the individual, when isolated, is not self-sufficing; and therefore he is like a part in relation to the whole. But he who is unable to live in society, or who has no need because he is sufficient for himself, must be either a beast or a god: he is no part of a state."[14] In Book IV Aristotle asserts that the individual virtues which

[12]   Plato, *The Laws* (628 C-D), trans. R. G. Bury, Loeb Library, 2 vols. (London & New York, 1924), I, 15-17. See also *Laws* (829 A), II, 127.
[13]   Aristotle, *The Politics* (1253a) trans. Benjamin Jowett, 2 vols. (Oxford, 1885), I, 4.
[14]   Aristotle, *Politics* (1253a), I, 4-5.

he described in the *Nicomachean Ethics* are identical with the ideal of a happy life for a city.[15] In other words, the individual is a valid microcosm of the *polis*. But Plato and Aristotle devote relatively little space to discussing the benefits the members derive from the body.

Several other instances of the use of the idea that a corrupt society is a diseased organism may be cited briefly. In Sophocles' *Antigone*, Teiresias says to Creon:

> And 'tis thy counsel that hath brought this sickness
> on our state.[16]

The *Wasps* of Aristophanes contains these lines:

> Hard were the task, and shrewd the intent, for a Comedy-
> poet all too great
> To attempt to heal an inveterate, old disease engrained
> in the heart of the state.[17]

The orations of Demosthenes were an attempt to rouse the public spirit of Athens against the danger of Philip of Macedon. In the Third Philippic, Demosthenes says that "Philip, like some course or attack of fever or some other disease is coming on those that yet seem very far removed."[18] On the other hand, imagery of disease is used to describe certain weaknesses in Philip's character which might be exploited: "For as in the human body, a man in health feels not partial ailments, but when illness occurs, all are in motion, whether it be a rupture or a sprain or anything else unsound; so with states and monarchs, whilst they wage external war, their weaknesses are undiscerned by most men, but the tug of a frontier war betrays all."[19] We are beginning to see the analogy of the body applied for a variety of purposes. A final example may be taken from Xenophon's *Memorabilia*, in which Socrates urges a reconciliation between two quarreling brothers: "What if a pair of hands refused the office of mutual help for which God made them, and tried to thwart each other; or if a pair of feet neglected the duty of working together, for which they were fashioned, and took to hampering each other? ... a pair of brothers, in my judgement, were made by

[15]   Aristotle, *Politics* (1295b), I, 126.
[16]   Sophocles, *Antigone* (1015), in: *Works*, trans. Richard C. Jebb (New York & Cambridge, 1940), p. 160.
[17]   Aristophanes, *Wasps* (650-51), in: *Aristophanes*, trans. Benjamin B. Rogers, Loeb Library, 3 vols. (London & New York, 1924), II, 471.
[18]   Demosthenes, *The Olynthiac and Other Public Orations*, trans. Charles R. Kennedy, Bohn's Library (London, 1865), p. 122.
[19]   Demosthenes, *Orations*, pp. 49-50.

God to render better service one to the other than a pair of hands and feet and eyes and all the instruments that he meant to be used as fellows."[20]

The idea of the body politic is made possible by Greek science, whose view of nature was generally accepted in Western thought until the Renaissance. The pre-Socratics formulated the doctrine of hylozoism, "that the world of nature is saturated or permeated by mind".[21] Moreover, as described in Plato's *Timaeus*, the universe was created according to the most perfect model: "the Cosmos, more than aught else, resembles most closely that Living Creature of which all other living creatures, severally and generically, are portions."[22] Thus the life and physiological order which an individual man possesses are in a sense identical with the life and order of the *polis* and the Cosmos. Because this ordered mind or life is present, science, including political science, is possible. This view of nature was almost continually threatened by some kind of materialism which would deny mind to matter; but until the seventeenth century, the challenge was never successful. It should also be kept in mind that Greek, like English and other modern languages, has two important meanings for the word 'nature' (*physis*). In one sense 'nature' is the sum of all created things. But it is also the defining principle of a thing or a type of things, as in the 'nature' or disposition of an individual or hardness as a quality of metal. Both of these meanings are relevant in a discussion of the idea of the body politic. The state is meaningfully like a human organism; each member of the state also has a useful function which is natural and appropriate both for the part and whole of which it is a part. Evidence is found in Aristotle:

The constitution of an animal must be regarded as resembling that of a well-governed city-state. For when order is once established in a city there is no need of a special ruler with arbitrary powers to be present at every activity, but each individual performs his own task as he is ordered, and one act succeeds another because of custom. And in animals the same process goes on because of nature, and because each part of them, since they are so constituted, is naturally suited to perform its own function; so

[20] Xenophon, *Memorabilia* (II.iii.18), trans. E. C. Marchant, Loeb Library (London and New York, 1923), p. 121.
[21] R. G. Collingwood, *The Idea of Nature* (Oxford, 1945), p. 3. See also Sabine, *History of Political Theory*, pp. 120-21.
[22] Plato, *Timaeus* (30), trans. R. G. Bury, Loeb Library (London & New York, 1929), p. 57. A recent treatment of these ideas is in the book by Leo Spitzer, *Classical and Christian Ideas of World Harmony*, ed. Anna G. Hatcher (Baltimore, 1963), pp. 8, 17 and *passim*.

that there is no need of soul in each part, but since it is situated in a central organ of authority over the body, the other parts live by their structural attachment to it and perform their own functions in the course of nature.[23]

Although the political application of the comparison between body and society appeared first in the Greek city-states, the comparison itself is not exclusively or originally Greek. Versions are found in the writings of many very early civilizations. The appearance of the analogy in India, Persia, Egypt, China, and elsewhere is probably part of man's desire to identify himself with his environment and thereby to control it. In the *Rig-Veda* (*ca.* 1500 B.C.) there is a hymn describing the gods' sacrifice of Purusa (man, or a personified world-soul) and the creation of the castes from his body:

> When they divided Purusa how many portions did they make?
> What do they call his mouth, his arms? What do they
> call his thighs and feet?
> The Brahman [priests] was his mouth, of both his arms
> was the Rajanya [warriors] made.
> His thighs became the Vaisya [shepherds], from his
> feet the Sudra [servants] was produced.[24]

An Indian debate analogous to the fable of the belly is found in the *Mahabharata*. The Mind claims that

The nose does not smell without me. (Without me) the tongue does not apprehend taste. The eye does not perceive color, the skin does not feel touch, the ear does not apprehend sound, when deprived of me. I am the eternal and foremost among all the elements.[25]

The senses reply that without them, the mind could not perceive or enjoy anything; arrogance is the product of ignorance.

The *polis* was only a shadow of its former self after the conquests of Alexander. At a banquet at Opis, Alexander prayed for *homonoia* between Macedonians and Persians; political thought entered a new era.[26] The idea of the individual and the idea of humanity were devel-

---

[23] Aristotle, *On the Movement of Animals* (703 a 30 ff.), trans. E. S. Forster, Loeb Library (Cambridge, Mass. & London, 1937), pp. 475-77. See also Collingwood, *Idea of Nature*, p. 43.

[24] *Rig-Veda* X.90 in: A. C. Clayton, *The Rig-Veda and Vedic Religion* (London & Madras, 1913), p. 166. The hymn goes on to describe the creation of the world and several gods from the body of Purusa. See also George P. Conger, "Cosmic Persons and Human Universes in Indian Philosophy", *Journal of the Asiatic Society of Bengal*, N.S. XXIX (1933), 255-70.

[25] *The Mahabharata* (XIV, xxii, 14-15), trans. Manmatha N. Dutt, 14 vols. (Calcutta, 1905), XIV, 27. Many other analogues are listed in *The Fables of Aesop*. ed. Joseph Jacobs, 2 vols. (London, 1889), I, 82-86.

[26] Sabine, *History of Political Theory*, pp. 141-45.

oped to help men learn to live in a political unit larger and more im-
personal than the *polis*. Because the idea of a body politic no longer
applied to the city-state, the thinkers of the Hellenistic period, especially
the Stoics, used the comparison to express the unity of a much larger
entity, whether it was one of the great monarchies or the whole universe
– mankind.[27] Some of the analogies which were created were more than
a little absurd. For example, Philo Judaeus used the language of a
physician and a diseased body (along with the figure of a pilot and a
ship) to urge the acceptance of disaster as the working out of divine
providence: "A physician treating serious and dangerous diseases sometimes amputates parts of the body, hoping to secure the health of the
rest. . . . No blame attaches . . . to the physician for the mutilation . . .
but on the contrary [he is] praised for looking to what is profitable
rather than what is pleasant, and for having done the right thing. In
the same way we must always reverence all-embracing nature and
acquiesce cheerfully in its actions in the universe. . . ."[28]

Some important statements of the body analogy appear among the
writings of the Roman Stoics. In *Of Offices* Cicero writes:

for if we will be so disposed that each for his own gain shall despoil or
offer violence to another, the inevitable consequence is, that the society of
the human race which is consistent with nature, will be broken asunder.
As, supposing each member of the body was so disposed as to think it
could be well if it should draw to itself the health of the adjacent member,
it is inevitable that the whole body would be debilitated and would perish;
so if each of us should seize for himself the interests of another, and wrest
whatever he could from each for the sake of his own emolument, the
necessary consequence is, that human society and community would be
overturned.[29]

Echoing Plato and Aristotle, Seneca repeats this in terms both of one's
country and of mankind:

To injure one's country is a crime; consequently also to injure a fellow
citizen – for he is a part of the country, and if we reverence the whole, the
parts are sacred – consequently to injure any man is a crime, for he is your
fellow-citizen in the greater commonwealth. What if the hands should desire
to harm the feet, or the eyes the hands? As all the members of the body
are in harmony one with another because it is to the advantage of the

[27] Nestle, "Die Fabel des Menenius Agrippa", p. 356.
[28] Philo Judaeus, *On Rewards and Punishments*, trans. F. H. Colson, in *Philo*,
10 vols., Loeb Library (Cambridge, Mass. & London, 1939-41), VIII, 331.
[29] Cicero, *Three Books of Offices*, (III.V.22) trans. Cyrus R. Edmunds, Harper's
Classical Library (New York, 1857), p. 122.

whole that the individual members be unharmed, so mankind should spare the individual man, because all are born for a life of fellowship, and society can be kept unharmed only by the mutual protection and love of its part.[30]

In the 95th Epistle to Lucilius, Seneca writes: "I can lay down for mankind a rule ... for our duties in human relationships: all that you behold, that which comprises both god and man, is one – we are all parts of one great body. Nature produced us related to one another, since she created us from the same source and to the same end."[31] The phrase "our duties in human relationships" is important for it shows the difference between the political thinking of the Stoics in Rome and the Greeks writing about the *polis*. Morality, including political morality, is conceived of in terms of one's relations with other individuals rather than in terms of membership in a *polis*. Under the Hellenistic monarchs and the Roman emperors, citizenship in the older Greek sense was impossible; political units were held together only by loyalty to a deified ruler.[32]

Among the expressions of the idea of a body politic developed in classical times is the fable of the belly. The early history of the fable is obscure, but it probably appeared in the fourth century along with a rather large group of politically didactic fables such as the flute player and the fish, and the dog and the sheep.[33] The earliest preserved version of the fable of the belly occurs in a prose collection attributed to Aesop:

The belly and the feet were arguing about their importance, and when the feet kept saying that they were so much stronger that they even carried the stomach around, the stomach replied, "But, my good friends, if I didn't take in food you wouldn't be able to carry anything."
So it it with armies too. Great numbers would mean nothing if the generals did not exercise good judgement.[34]

But this is only the germ of the fable; moreover, its application is very limited.

[30] Seneca, *On Anger* (II.xxxi.7-8), in *Moral Essays*, trans. John W. Basore, 3 vols., Loeb Library (London & New York, 1927-35), I, 235-37.
[31] Seneca, *Ad Lucilium Epistulae Morales*, trans. Richard M. Gummere, Loeb Library, 3 vols. (Cambridge, Mass. & London, 1917-43), III, 91.
[32] Sabine, *History of Political Theory*, pp. 146-47.
[33] Nestle, "Die Fabel des Menenius Agrippa," p. 352. Joseph Jacobs thought the fable was a genuine Roman folk fable (*The Fables of Aesop*, I, 88). See also Heinrich Gombel, "Die Fabel 'Vom Magen und den Gliedern' in der Weltliteratture", *Beihefte zur Zeitschrift für Romanische Philologie*, Heft 80 (Halle, 1934).
[34] *Aesop Without Morals*, trans. Lloyd W. Daly (New York & London, 1961), pp. 148, 282. The Greek text is given in Ben E. Perry, ed., *Aesopica* (Urbana, Ill., 1952), p. 371.

The fable does not appear to have been told by Phaedrus, Avianus, or Babrius – all of whom wrote Aesopic fables in verse. When the fable appears in the Roman historians – Livy, Dio Cocceianus, and Dionysius of Halicarnassus – it is given as an oration by the Senator Menenius Agrippa and is used to quell a rebellion of plebeians. According to the historians, the plebeians grew dissatisfied with senatorial rule after the expulsion of the Tarquins and withdrew from the city to the Mons Sacer. Menenius was sent by the Senate to urge them to return. In Livy Menenius is beloved by the people because he is one of them. He tells briefly the fable of the mutiny of the members against the allegedly idle belly. But when the belly is not fed, the whole body is reduced to weakness. It then becomes obvious that the belly "was no more nourished than it nourished the rest. . .".[35] The moral of the fable and its effects are succinctly stated: "Drawing a parallel from this to show how like was the internal dissension of the bodily members to the anger of the plebs against the Fathers, he prevailed upon the minds of his hearers."[36] As Nestle points out, the fable has a primitive, and therefore early and Greek tone; Livy mentions its *horrido modo* and begins it in a fabular manner: "*tempore quo in homine non, ut nunc, omnia in unum consentiant . . .*".[37]

A generation later the fable was retold by Dionysius of Halicarnassus, who did not use Livy as a source. Dionysius' version, more than three times longer, is embedded in a dull, rambling speech by Menenius. It is more detailed, more rhetorical, and the parallel between the rebellions against the belly and the Senate is very carefully spelled out: "Learn, therefore, plebeians, that just as in our bodies the belly thus evilly reviled by the multitude nourishes the body even while it is itself nourished, and preserves it while it is preserved itself . . . so in commonwealths the senate, which administers the affairs of the public and provides what is expedient for everyone, preserves, guards, and corrects all things."[38] Dionysius tells us that Menenius "is said to have related a kind of fable that he composed after the manner of Aesop . . ."[39] But Dionysius' elaborate narration has little Aesopic about it.

[35] *Livy* (II.xxxii.9-12), trans. B. O. Foster, Loeb Library, 14 vols., (London & New York, 1925-59), I, 325.
[36] *Livy*, I. 325.
[37] *Livy*, I, 322-24; Nestle, "Die Fabel des Menenius Agrippa", p. 353.
[38] Dionysius of Halicarnassus, *Roman Antiquities* (VI, lxxxvi), trans. Earnest Cary, Loeb Library, 7 vols. (Cambridge, Mass. & London, 1937-50), IV, 113.
[39] Dionysius, *Roman Antiquities*, IV, 101.

A century later, the fable appeared in Plutarch's *Life of Coriolanus*. Plutarch's Menenius is, if anything, briefer than Livy's, but the style and application are essentially the same. About A.D. 200 the historian Dio Cocceianus retold the fable in the concise style of Livy, but made some attempt to dramatize the dispute between the members and added the repentance by the members and the restoration of the body to health.[40]

From the later Stoics the idea of an organic society passed into the Christian tradition.[41] The most important passage is St. Paul's First Epistle to the Corinthians; it is sufficiently important to be quoted at length:

> For as the body is one, and hath many members, and all the members of that one body, being many, are one body: so also is Christ.
> For the body is not one member, but many.
> If the foot shall say, Because I am not the hand, I am not of the body; is it therefore not of the body?
> And if the ear shall say, Because I am not the eye, I am not of the body; is it therefore not of the body?
> If the whole body were an eye, where were the hearing? If the whole were hearing, where were the smelling?
> But now hath God set the members every one of them in the body, as it hath pleased him.
> And if they were all one member, where were the body?
> But now are they many members, yet one body.
> And the eye cannot say unto the hand, I have no need of thee: nor again the head to the feet, I have no need of you.
> Nay, much more those members of the body, which seem to be more feeble, are necessary:
> And those members of the body, which we think to be less honourable, upon these we bestow more abundant honour; and our uncomely parts have more abundant comeliness.
>
> That there should be no schism in the body; but that the members should have the same care one for another.
> And whether one member suffer, all the members suffer with it; or one member be honoured, all the members rejoice with it.
>
> (I. Cor. XII. 12, 14-23, 25-26)[42]

[40] Dio Cocceianus, *Roman History* (Bk. IV), trans. Earnest Cary, Loeb Library, 9 vols. (London & New York, 1914-27), I, 121-25. Since only fragments of extracts from the early books of Dio survive, his telling of the fable may have been more substantial. He was the chief source for the twelfth-century Byzantine chronicler Zonaras.

[41] Nestle, "Die Fabel des Menenius Agrippa", pp. 358-59; Nestle argues that St. Paul's use of the figure is conclusive evidence for his knowledge of Stoic doctrines.

[42] The analogy of the body is also used by St. Paul in I Cor. VI. 15-16 (which specifies love as the unifying force), x. 17; Eph. IV. 15-16; v. 30; and Rom. XII. 4-5.

The passage makes a number of points, many of which are familiar in the Stoics. It assumes a hierarchical order, established by God (or nature), of differentiated parts, all of which are necessary to the body and which ought not, therefore, to regard themselves as either independent of the body or as superior to the other members. More important is the identification of this body with Christ and those who follow Christ.

In the early centuries of Christianity, Paul's use of the organic analogy is repeated again and again as an admonition against disagreement and dissension among the Churches. In what is known as the Epistle to the Corinthians of I Clement (c. A.D. 96) this passage is found: "Let us take our body; the head is nothing without the feet, likewise the feet are nothing without the head; the smallest members of our body are necessary and valuable to the whole body, but all work together and are united in a common subjection to preserve the whole body."[43] The analogy is then applied to the situation in Corinth, where some Elders had been deposed: "Let, therefore, our whole body be preserved in Christ Jesus, and let each be subjected to his neighbor, according to the position granted to him."[44] Another example of the body analogy used to try to stop dissension in the Church is found in the letters of St. Basil. In a letter (A.D. 375) to a group in Pontus which had separated itself from the Church of Caesarea, Basil writes: "If you consider yourselves the head of the universal Church, the head cannot say to the feet: 'I have no need of you.' Or if you assign yourselves to another position among the ecclesiastical members, you cannot say to us who have been placed in the same body: 'We have no need of you.' For the hands need each other, and the feet steady each other, and it is through their working in concert that the eyes possess their clearness of perception."[45] Basil does not, in this use of St. Paul, refer to an established hierarchy; for his purposes the separatists can be the head or some other part of the body. He stresses the co-operative nature of the Church and the love (agape) which holds it together. In

[43]   In *The Apostolic Fathers*, trans. Kirsopp Lake, Loeb Library, 2 vols. (London & New York, 1912-13), I, 73.
[44]   *Apostolic Fathers*, I, 73. See also I, 89, in which Clement asks "Why do we divide and tear asunder the members of Christ, and raise up strife against our own body, and reach such a pitch of madness as to forget that we are members of another?" The analogy is briefly stated and similarly applied by Ignatius to the Trallians (*Apostolic Fathers*, I, 223).
[45]   Letter CCIII, in *The Letters of St. Basil*, trans. Roy J. Deferrari, Loeb Library, 4 vols. (London & New York, 1926-34), III, 149.

a letter to the Chalcidians, Basil uses the analogy to define the role of the clergy "as a head resting unharmed at the top and furnishing to the subordinate limbs of the body its own power of forethought. For as long as the eyes perform their particular function, the workings of the hands become skilled, and the movements of the feet occur without stumbling, and no part of the body is bereft of its befitting care."[46]

Not only did the early Churches have to face the problem of their relationship to each other; they had to define their relationship to the existing political order, the Roman Empire. From the beginning, respect for constituted authority was preached by the Christians following the words of Jesus to the Pharisees: "Render therefore unto Caesar the things which are Caesar's and unto God the things that are God's" (Matt. XXII. 21). St. Paul wrote to the Romans: "Let every soul be subject unto the higher powers. For there is no power but of God: The powers that be are ordained of God. Whosoever resisteth the power, resisteth the ordinance of God: and they that resist shall receive to themselves damnation" (Rom. XIII. 1-2; see also I Peter II. 13-17). God has imposed on Christians the duty of obedience to kings and magistrates. This obedience, moreover, is to the office, not the officer; even a bad ruler is "a minister of God, a revenger to execute wrath upon him that doeth evil" (Rom. XIII. 4).[47] Because the state maintains justice it is given this sacred power.

The significant fact about Christianity is that it divided men's loyalty between Caesar and God, when previously Caesar himself had been a god. In a sense this is a separation of man's interest in the physical and the spiritual, in the tradition of the Neo-Platonists. In another sense the concern for the spiritual is a withdrawal from a physical world in which meaningful individual action, including political action, is impossible; this withdrawal is seen in both Christian and pagan writers, such as Nero's tutor, Seneca. Yet the Church continued to exist in Caesar's empire; Christianity first gained toleration, then acceptance as the official religion of Rome. The relation of Church and state grew complex, the source of centuries of controversy. But the Fathers who discuss this relationship are not political philosophers;

---

[46] Letter CCXXII, in *Letters*, III, 285. See also letter LXVI (*Letters*, II, 31-33) in which Basil speaks of troubles in the Church at Antioch which prevent that church from giving health to the whole body of the Church.

[47] See also Sabine, *History of Political Theory*, pp. 180-83 and R. W. and A. J. Carlyle, *A History of Medieval Political Theory in the West*, 6 vols. (Edinburgh & London, 1903-36), I, 89-93.

they take ideas from the ancients and shape them to fit a Christian context.[48]

In our discussion of the early history of the idea of a body politic we may draw some sort of dividing line after the works of St. Augustine. After Augustine we encounter situations and problems which may more properly be called medieval, although I have neither the space nor the knowledge to define in detail this transition to the medieval in terms of the body politic. St. Augustine's *The City of God* was written to defend the Church against the charge that Christianity was responsible for Alaric's sack of Rome in A.D. 410.[49] The political views of this large scale apologia are often implicit rather than explicit, but they are important in Augustine's definition of the *Civitas terrena* and the *Civitas Dei*. Augustine assumes the unity of the human race and its essential sociability; the City of God can be described as the social life of the children of God.[50] The two cities cannot be identified with Church and State; both Church and State, which exist in the world of time, contain elements of the two cities which will be separated only on Judgment Day.[51] By no means does Augustine reject the State as totally given to sin; the State can do much good in the service of God. On occasion both Church and State are described in terms of a body. The Roman Empire, for example, consists of Rome "and those lands which . . . had by alliance or conquest become, as it were, members of the body of the state."[52] More important are the repeated descriptions of the Church (the *communio sanctorum*, not the ecclesiastical establishment) as the body of Christ: "Behold what the perfect man [Christ] is – the head and the body, which is made up of all the members, which in their own time shall be made perfected. But new additions are daily being made to this body while the Church is being built up, to which it is said, 'Ye are the body of Christ and His members'. . . ."[53] In another place Augustine speaks of "the spiritual body, which is already worn in anticipation by Christ as our head, and will be worn by his

---

[48] Carlyle, *Medieval Political Theory*, I, 195-96.
[49] For Augustine see Sabine, *History of Political Theory*, pp. 189-93; Carlyle, *Medieval Political Theory*, I, 125-28; and especially J. Neville Figgis, *The Political Aspects of S. Augustine's 'City of God'* (London, 1921).
[50] Figgis, *Political Aspects of . . . 'City of God'*, p. 38.
[51] Figgis, *Political Aspects of . . . 'City of God'*, pp. 51-80.
[52] St. Augustine, *The City of God* (III.i), trans. Marcus Dods (New York, 1950), pp. 74-75. Twice (pp. 121-22, 217) Augustine rejects the idea that God is the soul of the body of the world; such a notion lead to impiety.
[53] Augustine, *City of God* (XXII.18), p. 841.

members in the resurrection of the dead".[54] Moreover, Christ, the head of the Church, is without sin, but sins "are found in His body and members, which is his people".[55] The unity of this body is achieved through the sacraments: "For these have eaten the body of Christ, not only sacramentally but really, being incorporated in His body. . . ."[56] In these passages we see that the organic analogy is being applied for new purposes. The body being described is not the Athenian *polis* nor the Stoic universe nor an early Christian congregation, but it is the community of the saved, a community which has little real meaning in this world of time and mutability. We see here the idea of a mystical body (*corpus mysticum*) being developed. The later history of this idea takes us into the medieval period.

MEDIEVAL

With the disintegration of the Roman Empire in the West, there was almost complete cessation of explicitly political thinking.[57] In a period of increasing political, economic, and cultural disorder, men had little interest in speculating on the nature of warring tribes, baronies, and kingdoms. We must, therefore, turn to the Church to follow the idea of a body politic. The pronouncements of the medieval Church about its own nature are the thread which directly connects the political thought of antiquity with that of the Renaissance. These pronouncements are not political philosophy, but political theology; the difference is important. Our task in this section is to sketch the history of the organic analogy through the Middle Ages and, since this chapter is introductory to a study of the English Renaissance, to devote as much attention as is possible to the writings of Englishmen.

[54]   Augustine, *City of God* (XIII.21), pp. 434-35.
[55]   Augustine, *City of God* (XVII.9), p. 590.
[56]   Augustine, *City of God* (XXI.20), p. 791. See also pp. 582, 799.
[57]   For the medieval period I rely on R. W. Carlyle and A. J. Carlyle, *A History of Mediaeval Political Theory in the West*, 6 vols. (Edinburgh & London, 1903-36); Anton-Hermann Chroust, "The Corporate Idea and the Body Politic in the Middle Ages", *Review of Politics*, IX (1947), 423-52; Otto Gierke, *Political Theories of the Middle Age*, trans. Frederic W. Maitland (Cambridge, 1900); two volumes edited by F. J. C. Hearnshaw, *The Social and Political Ideas of Some Great Medieval Thinkers* (London, 1923), and *The Social and Political Ideas of Some Great Thinkers of the Renaissance and Reformation* (London, 1925); Ernst H. Kantorowicz, *The King's Two Bodies* (Princeton, 1951), esp. pp. 193-272; Ewart Lewis, "Organic Tendencies in Medieval Political Thought", *American Political Science Review*, XXXII (1938), 849-76; and Sabine, *History of Political Theory*, pp. 198-328.

The first work which should be mentioned, however, is the *Ency-clopedia* of the Arabic Brotherhood of Sincerity (*ca.* 950-1000). Al-though any influence which this work may have had on European tradition was indirect, the *Encyclopedia* is important because in it theories of microcosm and macrocosm are extensive and fundamental in contrast to the relatively fragmentary passages found previously.[58] Moreover it contains analogues of certain expressions found in later English writings. The human body is compared to a city; the relation of the senses to the soul parallels that of counsellors to a king. There is a long comparison of a body and the earth; bones correspond to mountains, marrow to minerals, plants to hair, and so forth. There are also astrological comparisons in which the planets are related to the organs and openings of the body, and the order of the stars to that of social and political relationships.

St. Paul's statement that "we are all of one body" was taken as a statement of the unity of Christian believers, "*Corpus Christi, quod est fidelium congregatio*", and was used as an exhortation to the practice of the Golden Rule. This application was used repeatedly in the devo-tional and didactic literature of the Middle Ages. A few examples may be quoted briefly. In the *Ancrene Riwle* (*ca.* 1200) there is a passage describing the suffering which Christians, like Christ, must endure: "nis God ure heaved and we alle his limes; and nis everich lim sor mid seoruwe of the heaved?"[59] A limb which does not sweat when the head sweats (as Christ sweated blood) is diseased and must be cut off. *The Pricke of Conscience*, once attributed to Richard Rolle, quotes St. Paul to explain charity:

> He says "we er alle als a body,"
> That has diverse lyms many.
> And als a lym of a body here
> Es redy, aftir it has powere,
> To serve alle the other, mar and les,
> Of that office that gyven it es,
> Right swa ilk man that here lyfes,
> Of all that God thurgh grace him gyfes,
> Sulk other serve, that thar-of has nede,
> Als he wille answere at the day of drede.[60]

[58] George P. Conger, *Theories of Macrocosms and Microcosms in the History of Philosophy* (New York, 1922), p. 50. I rely on Conger's sumary, pp. 46-52.
[59] *Ancrene Riwle*, ed. Mabel Day, EETS, O. S. 225 (London, 1952), p. 163.
[60] *The Pricke of Conscience*, ed. Richard Morris (Berlin, 1863), pp. 160-61, 11. 5926-35. See also Dan Michel of Northgate, *Ayenbite of Inwyt*, ed. Richard Morris, EETS, O. S. 23 (London, 1866), pp. 102 and 146-49 for elaborate de-scriptions of the love between the members of the body of Christ.

The finest religious poem in Middle English, the *Pearl*, contains a stanza in which the Maiden explains to the Dreamer that *courtaysye*, "courtesy" and "divine grace", prevents strife both in the kingdom of heaven and in the kingdom of this world:

> Of courtaysye, as saytʒ Saynt Poule,
> Al arn we membreʒ of Jesu Kryst:
> As heved and arme and legg and navle
> Temen to hys body ful trwe and tryste,
> Ryʒt so is uch a Krysten sawle .
> Alongande lym to the Mayster of myste.
> Thenne loke what hate other any gawle
> Is tached other tyʒed thy lymmeʒ bytwyste.
> Thy heved hatʒ nauther greme ne gryste,
> On arme other fynger thaʒ thou ber byʒe.
> So fare we alle wyth luf and lyste
> To kyng and quene by cortaysye.[61]

When schism afflicts the Church, says John Gower, all men suffer:

> Christ is the heved, and we ben membres alle,
> As wel the subjit as the sovereign;
> So sit it wel, that charite be plein. . . .
>
> Of that the heved is sick, the limes aken;
>   These regnes that to Christes pes belongen,
> Ffor worldes good these dedly werres maken,
>   Which heliples as in balance hongen.
>   The heved above hem hath noght undirfongen
> To sette pes, bot every man sleeth other.
> And in this wise hath charite no brother.[62]

It is the duty of kings to restore peace.

A corollary is the doctrine of work. Each part of the body has a function which must be performed; the lower classes are continually being urged to concentrate on their task of supporting the nobility and the clergy. "God has ordained three classes of men, namely labourers such as husbandmen and craftsmen to support the whole body of the Church after the manner of feet, knights to defend it in the fashion of hands, clergy to rule and lead it after the manner of eyes. And all the aforesaid who maintain their own status are of the family of God."[63]

---

[61]   *Pearl*, (11. 457-68), ed. E. V. Gordon (Oxford, 1953), p. 17.

[62]   John Gower, "Address of John Gower to Henry IV", *Political Songs and Poems*, ed. Thomas Wright, Rolls Series, 2 vols. (London, 1861), II, 9, 11.

[63]   John Bromyard, *Summa Predicantium*, quoted by G. R. Owst, *Literature and Pulpit in Medieval England* (Cambridge, 1933), p. 554. Owst lists the body analogy as one of many figures – husbandmen in a vineyard, architecture, etc. – used in

The body analogy is widely used in the conservative response to the literature of social and religious protest which appeared in England after 1350. Though the authors of such poems as *Wynner and Wastour* and *Piers Ploughman* criticize deviations from an ideal social order, the figure of the body politic seems to have been invoked only by those defending the *status quo*. A satire by "Jack Upland" against the friars was answered by "Friar Dan Topias":

> For right as in thi bodi, Jake,
> ben ordeyned thin hondis,
> for thin heed and for thi feet
> and for thin eyen to wirken,
> right so the comoun peple
> God hath disposid,
> to laboren for holi chirche
> and lordshipis also.[64]

Jack's answer is that Christ and the Apostles were willing to work with their hands.

This devotional and didactic use of the analogy continued more or less unchanged throughout the Middle Ages. But the analogy also found application in the more sophisticated literature of Church dogma and the great medieval struggles between Church and State. The mutations of the idea of a body politic through the centuries provide an interesting key to the religious and political history of the period.

During the early centuries of the Christian era a distinction was maintained between the *corpus Christi*, which was the Church, and the *corpus mysticum*, the Eucharist.[65] About the eighth century, these concepts began to fuse; the Eucharist became the element which mystically unified the Church.

Just as in a fine wheat flour which is brought together from many grains, so is the Church, which is a body of many members: ground between the mill stones of the Law and the Evangelists, dipped in the water of baptism, anointed with the oil of the chrism, joined together by the Holy Spirit.[66]

---

sermons and other didactic literature. I believe that the body analogy is probably the most common and certainly the most important of these.

[64] *Political Songs and Poems*, II 44-45.

[65] Kantorowicz, *The King's Two Bodies*, p. 195, relying heavily on Henri de Lubac, *Corpus Mysticum: L'Eucharistie et L'Eglise au Moyen Age*, 2nd. ed. (Paris, 1949), pp. 67-135.

[66] Bede, *Explanatio in Tertium Librum Mosis*, in: J. P. Migne, *Patrologiae Latina* (Paris, 1862), XCI, 334A. See Sister M. Thomas Carroll, *The Venerable Bede: His Spiritual Teachings*, Catholic University of America Studies in Medieval History, N.S. IX (Washington, 1946), esp. pp. 67-97.

This becomes traditional in handbooks of devotion such as the *Ayenbite of Inwyt*: "We byeth alle lemes of one bodye, huerof Iesu crist is thet heaved and we byeth the lemes, that we libbeth alle of onelepi mete, thet is of the holy vless and of the holy blod of Iesu crist thet ous zuo moche loveth. . . ."[67]

By the twelfth century, however, a reversal of terminology had taken place, due largely to the controversy about the meaning of transubstantiation; the Eucharist became the real body of Christ (*corpus naturale*) and the Church became the *corpus mysticum*.[68] Thus around 1200 Simon of Tournai writes: "Two are the bodies of Christ: the human material body which he assumed from the Virgin, and the spiritual collegiate body, the ecclesiastical college."[69] This is not the ancient distinction between the human and the divine natures of Christ, but is, as Gregory of Bergamo explained, "One body of Christ which is he himself, and another body of which he is the head".

More important for our purpose is the statement that the body of the Church is not just the community of believers, but is the ecclesiastical hierarchy whose head is the Pope. In the Middle Ages the Church was, or claimed to be, the supreme organization; the Church is the only state in which Empires and kingdoms are but constituent members.[70] In 1302, during the struggle with Philip the Fair of France, Pope Boniface VIII summarized the corporational doctrine of the Church in the bull *Unam Sanctam*: "We are compelled, our faith urging us, to believe and to hold . . . that there is one holy catholic and apostolic church . . . which represents one mystic body, of which body the head is Christ; but of Christ, God."[71] Papal supremacy over the Hohenstauffen Emperors had been won in these terms; the French were less interested in statements that "Just as all the limbs in the body natural refer to the head, so do all the faithful in the mystical body of the Church refer to the head of the Church, the Roman Pontiff".[72]

---

[67]   *Ayenbite of Inwyt*, ed. Morris, p. 146.
[68]   Kantorowicz, *The King's Two Bodies*, pp. 196-97; Lubac, *Corpus Mysticum*, pp. 87-88.
[69]   Quoted by Kantorowicz, *The King's Two Bodies*, p. 108.
[70]   John N. Figgis, *Political Thought From Gerson to Grotius*, 2nd ed (Cambridge, 1916), p. 5. The history of the papal claims is traced by Walter Ullman, *The Growth of Papal Government in the Middle Ages*, 2nd ed. (London, 1962).
[71]   *Unam Sanctam*, in: *Select Historical Documents of the Middle Ages*, trans. Ernest F. Henderson (London, 1896), p. 435. For an extended summary of papal claims see Michael Wilks, *The Problem of Sovereignty in the Later Middle Ages* (Cambridge, 1963), pp. 15-64.
[72]   Hermann of Schilditz, quoted by Kantorowicz, *The King's Two Bodies*, p.

In the phrase "mystical body of the Church" (*corpus Ecclesiae mysticum*) St. Thomas Aquinas carried the development of the idea one step further; the Church not only represented the mystical body of Christ, but the Church itself was a mystical body.[73] Aquinas examines the organic analogy in detail:

In the natural body is found a quadruple union of the members to one another. The first is according to the conformity of nature, because all members consist of the same like parts .... even as the hand and foot [are] of flesh and bone.... The second is through the binding of them to one another by nerves and joints; and thus they are called one by continuity. The third is according as the vital spirit and forces of the soul are diffused through the whole body. The fourth is according as all members are perfected by the soul.... And these four unions are found in the mystic body. The first, inasmuch as all its members are of one nature either in genus or species. The second, inasmuch as they are bound to one another by faith, because they are continuous in the thing believed. The third, according as they are vivified by grace and love. The fourth, according as in them is the Holy Spirit, who is the ultimate and principal perfection of the whole mystic body, like the soul in the natural body.[74]

The end of the individual is the same as those of the organizations of which he is a part, the Church and the State; these organizations exist for his sake. Aquinas recognizes both secular and spiritual authority and asserts the superiority of the spiritual, the Papal: "As the body has being, power, and action by reason of the soul ... so also the temporal jurisdiction of princes by reason of the spiritual jurisdiction of Peter and his successors."[75]

The supremacy of the Papacy, as head of the Church was used, with varying degrees of success, to censure and depose secular rulers. In fact the Middle Ages placed, often hesitatingly, a variety of limitations

---

203. See also Isaac of Stella, Sermon XXXIV, in: Migne, *Patrologiae Latina* (Paris, 1855), CXCIV, 1801C ff. and Jonas of Orleans, *De Institutione Regia*, in: Migne, *Patrologiae Latina* (Paris, 1864), CVI, 285 B: "It is known to all the faithful that the universal Church is the body of Christ and that its head is Christ and in it are two principles, the priestly and the royal, and the priestly is so much superior that reason is given through them to the kings."

[73] Kantorowicz, *The King's Two Bodies*, p. 201, stresses the juristic nature of this language. See also Lubac, *Corpus Mysticum*, pp. 127-28, esp. the references in the notes.

[74] Aquinas, *Commentary on the Sentences of Peter Lombard*, quoted by Lewis, "Organic Tendencies in Medieval Political Thought", pp. 858-59. See also E. Aveling, "St. Thomas and the Papal Monarchy," in: *Social and Political Ideas of Some Great Medieval Thinkers*, ed. Hearnshaw, p. 102.

[75] Aquinas, *De Regimine Principum*, quoted by Aveling, "St. Thomas and the Papal Monarchy", p. 102, n. 2.

on the authority and security of princes. The Teutonic tradition of elective kingship provided some sort of justification for deposing princes
who oppressed their subjects.[76] The Church, following St. Paul,
preached obedience to secular rulers as ordained of God, but sometimes exceptions had to be made. A heretical or schismatic king could
not, theoretically, be tolerated. Sometimes Churchmen admitted other
valid causes for deposing a king. Aquinas wrote that a tyrant, one interested in his own welfare and not that of his subjects, was himself
guilty of the sin of sedition and that removing him by force was justifiable.[77] The theoretical right of popular rebellion was generally admitted
under certain conditions; in practice rebellion was a different matter.[78]

The great thinkers of the Middle Ages – Aquinas, Dante, John of
Salisbury – all visualized a great world community, unified and at
peace, striving for the salvation of men's souls. Dante's *De Monarchia*,
though it was out of touch with reality before it was written, is a
magnificent statement of the medieval obsession for harmony and
order in Church and State. But there were other forces at work, forces
embodying a different kind of political consciousness which in time
rendered meaningless the ideals of unity and hierarchical authority
enunciated in the *Unam Sanctam*. The conflict between the Papacy and
the emerging national monarchies resulted in the appropriation of the
language of political theology by the secular princes, especially the new
use of the metaphor of the body politic to describe these monarchies.
The phrase *corpus politicum* grew increasingly popular in the thirteenth
century; the rediscovery and translation of Aristotle's *Politics* (1260)
was probably an important factor in this process.[79]

There were three possible responses to Papal claims of headship of
the universal order. One could admit the Papal claims and then identify
king or emperor with the heart and stress the importance of this organ
to the head. Or one could define a secular body, a *corpus naturale*

---

[76] Carlyle and Carlyle, *Mediaeval Political Theory*, I, 210-11, 249-50. See also
Fritz Kern, *Kingship and Law in the Middle Ages*, trans. S. B. Chrimes (Oxford,
1939), esp. pp. 69-133.
[77] *Summa Theologica*, trans. Dominican Fathers, 3 vols. (New York, 1947), II,
1366 (II-II, Quest. 42).
[78] For a general survey see Wilfred Parsons, "The Medieval Theory of the Tyrant", *The Review of Politics*, IV (1942), 129-43. Magna Carta established some
elaborate machinery to remove temporarily the king's power while certain grievances were being corrected. Magna Carta did not go so far as to create procedure
for deposition; in practice the constitutional machinery for correcting abuses did
not work. See Kern, *Kingship and Law*, pp. 127-33.
[79] Kantorowicz, *The King's Two Bodies*, p. 225.

distinct from the *corpus mysticum* of the Church, which had its own head yet was not monstrously two-headed or schizophrenic. Finally, and most radically, one could maintain that only Christ, and not the Pope, was the *caput Ecclesiae*.[80] The Avignon captivity may be regarded as one consequence of the second view; the third leads finally to the Reformation and the establishment of national churches.

Though written almost a century and a half before *Unam Sanctam*, the *Policraticus* of John of Salisbury is of considerable interest in the development of the theory of the secular state. The *Policraticus* is the first extended attempt to write political philosophy in the Middle Ages, and the only one before the rediscovery of Aristotle's *Politics*.[81] John's discussion is not of a feudal society, but of a *res publica* in the tradition of Cicero. The framework of this discussion is an elaborate comparison of the state and the human body which John alleges to be taken from Plutarch's *Institutio Trajani*.[82] "A commonwealth . . . is a certain body which is endowed with life by the benefit of divine favor, which acts at the prompting of the highest equity. . . ."[83] After identifying the soul of the body with the ministers of God, John devotes several brief chapters to the respect due religion, but he says nothing explicit about the powers of the Papacy.

The prince is the head of the body, subject only to God and (in general terms) to those who represent God on earth. The great bulk of John's analysis is devoted to the members of the body – the heart (Senate), hands (soldiers and officials), stomach (financial officers) and the feet (the tillers of the soil).[84] The relative positions of the members of this hierarchy are fixed so that there is no active political participation by the inferior members of the body. But he is aware to an unusual degree of the need for spiritual unity within the state. Not only must the feet labor to support and protect the head, but the prince must

---

[80] Lubac, *Corpus Mysticum*, pp. 130-31.

[81] The most important portions have been translated by John Dickinson as *The Statesman's Book* (New York, 1927); see also Dickinson, "The Mediaeval Conception of Kingship as Developed in the *Policraticus* of John of Salisbury", *Speculum*, I (1926), 307-37; E. F. Jacob, "John of Salisbury and the *Policraticus*", in: *Social and Political Ideas of Medieval Thinkers*, ed. Hearnshaw, pp. 53-84; Kantorowicz, pp. 94-97; Sabine, pp. 246-47; and Clement C. J. Webb, *John of Salisbury* (London, 1932).

[82] This Pseudo-Plutarch is identified with John himself by H. Liebeschuetz, "John of Salisbury and Pseudo-Plutarch", *Journal of the Warburg and Courtauld Institutes*, VI (1943), 33-39.

[83] John of Salisbury, *Statesman's Book*, p. 64.

[84] John of Salisbury, *Statesman's Book*, p. 65.

inspire "the affection of all that for his sake every subject will expose his own head to imminent dangers in the same manner that by the promptings of nature the members of the body are wont to expose themselves for the protection of the head."[85] In a work so filled with discussion of the body politic, it is not surprising to find the fable of the belly, which John says he learned in Rome from Pope Adrian IV. John's version is longer than that of Livy, but not nearly so involved as that of Dionysius of Halicarnassus. The moral of the fable is that "in the body of the commonwealth, wherein, though the magistrates are most grasping, yet they accumulate not so much for themselves as for others".[86] Therefore the people should not challenge the exactions of Popes and princes. It is interesting to note that John does not hesitate to let the prince in one chapter (V, 2) be the head of the commonwealth and in another (VI, 24) the belly.

In spite of his statements about the organic nature of a commonwealth and a belief that rebellion is sacrilege, John draws a distinction between a lawful prince and a tyrant who ignores the law or attacks religion, and describes a tyrannical state in terms of a diseased body. He goes to the extreme of defending tyrannicide, even by an individual citizen. It should be pointed out, however, that John seems to have shied away from urging the death of tyrants such as Frederick Barbarossa, who supported an anti-Pope.[87] Although John discusses the body politic in elaborate detail, even extravagant detail, it is not clear whether he is talking about the Empire, a nation, a province, or something else. But whatever the reason for this vagueness, there does seem to be a definite secular orientation in the *Policraticus*, which is a little surprising when one considers that its author was Bishop of Chartres and a close friend of Thomas à Becket.

John of Salisbury's use of the fable of the belly makes this an appropriate place to consider the history of the fable through the Middle Ages. It is contained in the Aesopic collection attributed to Romulus Vulgaris, who in general follows the Latin fabulist Phaedrus.[88] Although

85 John of Salisbury, *Statesman's Book*, p. 17.
86 John of Salisbury, *Statesman's Book*, p. 257.
87 Webb, *John of Salisbury*, pp. 66-67.
88 The standard collection of medieval Latin fables in Léopold Hervieux, *Les Fabulists Latins*, 5 vols. (Paris, 1884-99). The text of Romulus' version of the fable of the belly is in II, 213; Hervieux follows a tenth century MS. See also George Thiele, *Der lateinische Äsop des Romulus* (Heidelberg, 1910), pp. 220-222. From medieval prose texts Karl Zander reconstructed a fable in verse that Phaedrus might have written (*Phaedrus Solutus* [Lund, 1921], pp. 16-19).

Romulus' version is short, its language shows no trace of the influence of Livy, thus indicating a separate tradition among the collections of fables.

No one is strong without a part of himself, as with the parts of the human body, of whom it is said the Hand and Feet were angry, and did not wish to give the belly food, which without work was filled again daily, sitting at leisure. In turn the Hand and Feet did not wish to work and refused to do so. The belly, in truth, clamored with hunger. But for a few days these would give it nothing. The spirits of the members, however, grew weak because of the belly. Afterwards, in truth, the belly refused to take food willingly, because the ways were now closed. So the Members and the Belly, exhausted, perished together.

From this source the fable was retold in prose and verse in many languages throughout Europe.[89] Some of the fables found their way into the *Speculum Historiale* of Vincent of Beauvais.[90] Although England was a center for the writing of Aesopic fables, as is shown by the collections of Walter of England and Alexander Neckham and the lost version attributed to King Alfred, there are no surviving collections of fables in English before the translations made by Caxton late in the fifteenth century.[91] In general the fables are brief although some of the French versions run to eighty short verses. Frequently a simple, but not explicitly political, moral is attached:

> So he who condems gifts appropriate for life
> Is warned by loss to obey them in return.[92]

Fifteenth-century English writings contain several examples of the fable of the belly used in political writings for political purposes. England was sufficiently engrossed with the Wars of the Roses so that the Conciliar movement was more or less ignored. This isolation of

---

[89] See the texts in Hervieux, *Les Fabulists Latins*, II, 169, 272, 325, 353-54, 379, 464, etc. French versions are edited by Wendelin Foerster, *Lyoner Yzopet*, Altfranzosische Bibliothek, V (Heilbronn, 1882), 79-80; and Kenneth McKenzie and William A. Oldfather, *Ysopet-Avionnet*, University of Illinois Studies in Language and Literature, V (Urbana, 1919), 162-64; and Julia Bastin, *Recuil Genèral des Isopets*, SATF, 2 vols. (Paris, 1929-30), I, 100-103, 165-169; II, 179-181, 299-302. Four medieval Italian versions are in *The Isopo Laurenziana*, ed. Muray P. Brush (Baltimore, 1898), pp. 54-56.

[90] Hervieux, *Les Fabulists Latins*, II, 243; English translation by Caxton, 1481.

[91] Texts of Walter and Neckham are in Hervieux, *Les Fabulists Latins*, II, 412, 807. See also E. Mall, "Zur Geschichte der Mittelalterlichen Fabelliteratur und insbesondere des Esope der Marie de France", *Zeitschrift für Romanische Philologie*, II 1885), 191-93. For a full history of the fable literature of the Middle Ages, see *Aesops levned og fabler*, ed. Bengt Holbek, 2 vols. (Copenhagen, 1961).

[92] Alexander Neckham, in Hervieux, *Les Fabulists Latins*, II, 807.

England produced a turning in, a rapidly growing concern for exclusively English political problems. The references to the body politic in fifteenth-century England show, therefore, an increasingly specific analysis of the English body politic and the relegation of the clergy to an appropriate place within the hierarchy of the English nation. In effect, I am arguing that the use of the organic analogy indicates a frame of mind anticipating Henry VIII's break with Rome and his establishing himself as head of both Church and State.

An interesting example of the description of society in terms of the parts of the body combined with the fable of the belly is "The Descryvyng of Mannes Membres", one of the early fifteenth-century poems in Oxford MS. Digby 102.[93] The poem is divided into nineteen eight-line stanzas. The first ten compare the parts of a body to the classes of a kingdom:

> The heved, y likne to a king,
>   For he is lord sovereyn of al,
> Hath foure to his governyng:
>   Mouth and nose, and eyen with-al,
> Eryn fayre to his heryng,
>   To serve the brayn is pryncypal
> Chef of counseil ymagenyng,
>   To caste before, er after fal.   (11. 9-16)

The breast is likened to a priest; there is no suggestion of priestly authority over the king, although the breast is regarded as the resting place of the soul.[94] The neck is a judge, the arms are knights, the fingers are yeomen, the ribs are men of law, the thighs are merchants, the feet are ploughmen, and the toes are faithful servants. All serve useful functions:

> Toes helpeth man fro fal to ryse.
> He may not stonde, that hath no toon.
>
> And maystres, though they ben wyse,
> Without-out servant lyve not alon.   (11. 73-74, 79-80)

---

[93]   Poem XV in *Twenty-Six Political and Other Poems*, ed. J. Kail, EETS O.S. 124 (London, 1904), pp. 64-69. Curiously, Kail's long introduction fails to comment on this poem.

[94]   Another example of this tendency to make the Church a part of the body of the realm is found in a sermon to Parliament in 1404 in which Bishop Beaufort "compared a realm to the body of a man, the right side of which he compared to the Holy Church, and the left side to the Temporal Lords, and the other members to the Commons ...". These three estates are summoned to Parliament to give "advice, counsel and general assent" to their lord the King. Quoted by S. B. Chrimes, *English Constitutional Ideas in the Fifteenth Century* (Cambridge, 1936), p. 116.

Then follows a fable in which the womb (a bottomless purse, Parliament?), the eyes, the feet and the other members of the body protest that the mouth is too gluttonous and ask it to stop eating for three days. The mouth angrily agrees. At the end of the three days, the much weakened parts of the body plead with the mouth to resume eating. The mouth says they are fickle, to which the hands and feet reply:

> "We may play, swynke, and swete,
>   While mouthe in mesure maketh his mele.
> For mesure kepeth kynde hete,
>   And al that tyme we fare wele."   (ll. 117-120).

Presumably the fable represents a plea by the Commons for some kind of fiscal moderation by Henry IV or Henry V. By altering the traditional fable so that the members rebel against the mouth instead of the belly, the poem achieves a kind of consistency which was lacking in the *Policraticus*. There follows a comparison of peace in a kingdom with harmony in a human body and an obscure admonition that a kingdom (England?) which has lost its friends (Flanders?) must avoid its enemies (France?). The poem is far from perfect. The transitional stanza (11) is not clear, nor are the final stanzas. But with its concern for specifically English problems, the poem is representative of the fifteenth-century use of the organic analogy.

In Lydgate's *Fall of Princes* there is a chapter describing the dependence of rulers on their subjects, like a statue which cannot stand without legs and feet. Nature has set all the parts in true order and proportion:

> The hed set hiest be custom, as men knowe,
> The bodi amyd, the feet beneth lowe.[95]

The prince is the head, whose reason and clear foresight "Ther feet preserve that thei erre nouht". The knights are the arms and hands who protect the church, widows, and maidens. Judges are the eyes; the torso is made up of officials, burgesses, and merchants. The clergy, "folk contemplatiff", are the life-giving soul. Bearing up and sustaining the body are the laborers, the legs and feet. The point of this chapter is that

> . . . as a bodi which that stant in helthe
> Feelith no greeff off no froward humours,
> So everi comoun contynueth in gret welthe,

[95] John Lydgate, *The Fall of Princes*, ed. Henry Bergen. EETS, E.S. 121 (London, 1924), p. 222.

> Which is demened with prudent governours,
> That can appese debatis and errours,
> The peeple keepe from al contraversie,
> Causying ther weelfare tencrece & multeplie.[96]

Among the more interesting political documents of the late fifteenth century are three drafts of a sermon which Bishop John Russell prepared for the Parliaments of Edward V (which were never held) and Richard III.[97] The third of these drafts brings together elements from the first two to produce what is almost an encyclopedia of the discussions of the body politic in medieval literature. As part of an exhortation to unity, obedience, and work, Russell begins with a reference to St. Paul, "who lykkene the mistyk or the politike body of congregacione of peuple to the naturalle body of man . . .".[98] The use of the word "mistyk" is a clear example of the thoroughness of the borrowing of theological terminology for the purposes of secular politics. Russell then quotes Pomponius' definitions of three types of bodies: "Oon undir oo spirit, as a manne . . . a stone. An othir aggregate of dyverse thynges ioyned to gedir by nayle, cement, or other wise, as a house, a schyppe. The iijd oon body resultynge of dyverse bodyes to gedyr assecrate, and yet eche distaunt from othyr, as a flokke, a peuple, a College, a cite, a Reaulme."[99] These bodies all must be cared for: "The thynge public of a Realme or citee ys alle wey as hyt were a chylde with yn age, undir warde tutle or cure and tuicion of such as have the governaunce of the comine."[100] After listing the three estates, the principal members under the head "of thys grete body of Englonde", gathered in Parliament, Russell tells the fable of the belly, not as a past-tense narrative but in the form of a present conjecture:

[96]   Lydgate, *Fall of Princes*, p. 223. See also a sermon preached in 1373 by Thomas Brinton, Bishop of Rochester: "In this Mystical Body there are many members, because the heads are the kings, princes, and prelates; the eyes are wise judges and true councillors; the ears are religious; the tongue, good doctors; the right hand is the soldiers ready to defend; the left hand is the merchants and faithful mechanics; the heart is the citizens and burghers placed in the centre; the feet are the farmers and labourers supporting the whole body firmly." (Thomas Brinton, *The Sermons of Thomas Brinton, Bishop of Rochester*, ed. Sister Mary Aquinas Devlin, 2 vols., Camden Society, 3rd ser., LXXXV-LXXXVI [London, 1954], I, xxiii, Latin text, p. 111).

[97]   Chrimes, *English Constitutional Ideas*, pp. 168-91.

[98]   Chrimes, *English Constitutional Ideas*, p. 185. For another association of St. Paul and Aesop, see Jean Gerson's sermon "Vade in domum tuam" (1397), *Oeuvres complètes*, ed. Palémon Glorieux, 11 vols. (Paris, 1960), V, 576.

[99]   Chrimes, *English Constitutional Ideas*, p. 186.

[100]   Chrimes, *English Constitutional Ideas*, p. 187.

"for yf the fete and hondes . . . wolde compleyne agaynste the wombe . . . they and alle the othir membres schulde nedes perishe to gedyr."[101] As in the *Policraticus* the king can be both head and belly. The sermon concludes with some comments on one who incites the people to rebellion being a "roten membre" of the body politic.[102]

In spite of the turmoil and turbulence of the Wars of the Roses, fifteenth-century England produced one important figure in the history of political thought. Sir John Fortescue is the first to give a tentative literary expression to the idea that, constitutionally, England is a parliamentary monarchy. He introduces realistic observations of existing conditions into a theoretical discussion of government.[103] Fortescue's most important writing is the *De Laudibus Legum Anglie* (1468-71). The *De Laudibus* is a dialogue between young Prince Edward and the chancellor (Fortescue) to the exiled Henry VI. The chancellor urges the Prince not to devote all his time to military training but also to study the laws of England to enable him to render justice to his subjects. Fortescue praises the laws of England by comparing them in specific detail to the civil (Roman) law, and he patriotically asserts the superiority of the English polity to the French. Fortescue recognizes three forms of government: *dominium regale, dominium politicum*, and *dominium politicum et regale*. Although *dominium politicum* is slighted in the *De Laudibus*, the difference between regal, and political and regal dominion is important in Fortescue's comparison of England and France. The French king, who rules *regale*, permits his men-at-arms to pillage the villages, levies excessive taxes, and generally oppresses the people through such impositions as his salt monopoly. "Exasperated by these and other calamities, the people live in no little misery."[104] But under the rule of a king governing politically and regally, the English people enjoy unmatched happiness and prosperity.[105] The most

---

[101] Chrimes, *English Constitutional Ideas*, p. 188.

[102] Chrimes, *English Constitutional Ideas*, p. 189.

[103] S. B. Chrimes, Introduction to Fortescue's *De Laudibus Legum Anglie* (Cambridge, 1942), pp. ci-cii. See also Arthur B. Ferguson, "Fortescue and the Renaissance: a Study in Transition," *Studies in the Renaissance*, VI (1959), 175-94; Felix Gilbert, "Sir John Fortescue's *Dominium Regale et Politicum*", *Medievalia et Humanistica*, II (1944), 87-97; E. F. Jacob, "Sir John Fortescue and the Law of Nature", *Bulletin of the John Rylands Library*, XVIII (1934), 359-76; A. E. Levett, "Sir John Fortescue", in: *Some Social and Political Ideas of the Renaissance and the Reformation*, ed. Hearnshaw, pp. 61-85; and R. W. K. Hinton, "English Constitutional Theories: Sir John Fortescue to Sir John Eliot", *English Historical Review*, LXXV (1960), 410-25.

[104] Fortescue, *De Laudibus Legum Anglie*, ed. Chrimes, p. 83.

[105] Fortescue, *De Laudibus*, pp. 87, 89.

important section of the *De Laudibus* for our consideration is the description of the origins of these contrasting types of government (chapters XII and XIII).

Regal dominion is essentially absolutely monarchy.

Formerly men excelling in power, greedy of dignity and glory, subjugated neighboring peoples to themselves, often by force, and compelled them to serve them, and to submit to their commands, to which in time they themselves gave sanction as laws for these people.[106]

The essence of regal power is force and greed and usurpation; Nimrod, Bellus, the Romans, and indeed most other rulers, have founded their states in this manner. Fortescue rejects the notion that regal dominion is most similar to the divine and therefore best. He feels that there is too great a temptation for a good king to rule according to his personal whims and thereby become an irresponsible tyrant, as in the case of France.

The King of England rules regally and politically, but the regal aspects of this rule are emergency powers to meet surprise invasions and initiative in government policy. In defining the political aspects of the king's authority Fortescue has recourse to the analogy of the body politic. He begins with a quotation from St. Augustine defining a people as a body united by community of interest and consent to law.[107]

But such a people does not deserve to be called a body whilst it is acephalous, i.e. without a head. ... So a people wishing to erect itself into a kingdom or any other body politic [*corpus politicum*], must always set up one man for the government of all that body, who by analogy with a kingdom is ... usually called a king. As in this way the physical body grows out of the embryo, regulated by one head, so the kingdom issues from the people and exists as a body mystical [*corpus mysticum*], governed by one man as head.[108]

As in Bishop Russell's sermon, Fortescue uses the theological term 'mystical body' to describe a kingdom. Fortescue is not seriously interested in any state which is not a kingdom; he scarcely considers such a thing possible. The definition from Augustine is applied in terms of the anthropomorphic analogy. Like the head, "in the body politic the will of the people is the source of life, having in it the blood, namely, political forethought for the interest of the people, which it transmits to the head and all the members of the body ...".[109] The law is likened

---

106   Fortescue, *De Laudibus*, p. 29.
107   Fortescue, *De Laudibus*, p. 31.
108   Fortescue, *De Laudibus*, p. 31.
109   Fortescue, *De Laudibus*, p. 31.

to the nerves which unite the body politic. "And just as the head of the body physical is unable to change its nerves, or to deny its members proper strength and due nourishment of blood, so a king who is head of the body politic is unable to change the laws of that body, or to deprive that same people of their own substance uninvited or against their wills."[110]

The 'medieval commonplace' of the body politic went, as we have seen, through a series of permutations. Originating as an expression of the unity of the Greek *polis*, it became in turn an important concept in the intellectual arsenals of Stoic philosophers, Christian theologians, and spokesmen for the rising monarchies of late medieval Europe. It was used in writings of varying degrees of sophistication, from Papal bulls to philosophic essays to doggerel verses. Throughout this long and varied history the fundamental view of nature on which the validity of the analogy rested remained unchanged. Man accepted, in general, a view which saw the universe, the world, the church, the state, and the individual, repeating the same pattern of arrangement and therefore exhibiting precise correspondences. All of these levels of being were, moreover, permeated with a life or soul of their own, giving meaning and order to the data of existence. The English Renaissance witnessed the final flourishing of the idea of the body politic, while at the same time it produced the variety of challenges to the anthropomorphic view of the universe, challenges which eventually wrought a profound change on man's understanding of himself and his environment to produce that perplexing world view which we call 'modern'.

---

[110] Fortescue, *De Laudibus*, pp. 31, 33.

III

THE EARLY TUDORS

The passages examined at the end of the preceding chapter form a necessary background for Henry VIII's declaration that "this realm of England is an empire . . . governed by one Supreme Head and King . . . unto whom a body politic, compact of all sorts and degrees of people . . . be bounden and owe to bear next to God a natural and humble obedience".[1] Through this act and others like it the idea of the body politic was applied in a new context. By denying Papal Supremacy and proclaiming himself "Supreme Head of the Church of England", the king laid himself open to the charge that he had destroyed the unity of the Church Universal, the mystical body of Christ. Henry and his supporters had on the one hand to deny the claims of the Pope and on the other to maintain the royal headship and the organic unity of the Church *of* England as contrasted to the Church *in* England. The situation was further complicated by conservative resistance to the break with Rome and the slowly increasing trickle of radical notions coming from the Continent which combined with the native tradition of Lollardy to produce a demand for a more thorough reformation. The unity of the English body politic was repeatedly invoked to stave off rebellion and the threat of rebellion. Economic, rather than religious, grievances lay behind not a little of the national uneasiness. A number of writers, many of them humanists, responded to this situation by analyzing, often in terms of a diseased body, contemporary social and economic conditions.

Defense of royal supremacy, discouragement of popular or aristocratic rebellion, the portrayal of the problems of the realm – these were the specific purposes to which the analogy of the body politic was put.

---

[1] 24 Henry VIII c. 12, *Tudor Constitutional Documents: A.D. 1485-1603*, ed. J. R. Tanner (Cambridge, 1922), p. 41. Cf. the anachronistic claim in Shakespeare's *King John*, III.i.155-60, in: *The Complete Plays and Poems of William Shakespeare*, ed. William A. Neilson and Charles J. Hill (Cambridge, Mass., 1942).

A good deal of this appears to be simply the application of old language to express old answers to problems of almost equal antiquity. It is true that the medieval opponents of the Papacy supplied much useful ammunition to the supporters of Henry VIII; Marsilius of Padua's *Defensor Pacis* (1324) is a case in point.[2] But not even the simplest idea can cross one continent and two centuries without significant change.

Throughout the early sixteenth century the idea of the organic unity of the state was widely proclaimed. One of the *Epigrams* (1518) of Thomas More says that

A kingdom in all its parts is like a man; it is held together by natural affection. The king is the head; the people form the other parts. Every citizen the king has he considers a part of his own body (that is why he grieves at the loss of a single one). His subjects exert themselves in the king's behalf, and they all look upon him as the head for which they provide the body.[3]

A few years later, Sir Thomas Elyot began *The Boke Named the Governour* with a definition: "A publike weale is a body lyvyng, compacte or made of sondry estates and degrees of men, which is disposed by the order of equite and governed by the rule and moderation of reason."[4] Such brief statements were especially appropriate in the first three decades of the century, before Henry VIII's divorce and its consequences raised some painfully specific questions about the nature of the mystical and political bodies to which a man might belong.

These questions were not first asked in England, but at Wittenberg, when Luther's doubts about the efficacy of indulgences led to doubts about the Pope's headship of the body of Christ and a reliance on the authority of secular princes. The first English reaction to Luther was an affirmation of the traditional unity of the Church. John Fisher, Bishop of Rochester, quoted St. Paul that a woman had three spiritual heads – God, Christ, and her husband – in addition to her own natural head: "It were a monstrous syght to se a woman withouten an heed; what comforte sholde hyr housbande have upon hyr."[5] We are not to imagine

---

[2] For Marsilius' influence on Starkey see Franklin Le V. Baumer, "Marsilius of Padua and Thomas Starkey", *Politics*, II (1936), 188-205.

[3] Epigram 94. *The Latin Epigrams of Thomas More*, trans. Leicester Bradner and Charles A. Lynch (Chicago, 1953), p. 172; Latin text, p. 49.

[4] Thomas Elyot, *The Boke Named the Governour*, ed. Henry H.S. Croft, 2 vols. (London, 1880), I, 1.

[5] John Fisher, "Sermon Made Agayn the Pernicyous Doctryn of Martin Luther", (1521), *The English Works of John Fisher*, ed. John E. B. Mayor, EETS, E.S. 27 (London, 1876), p. 321.

a monstrosity with four similar heads attached to one neck; the head-body analogy describes a hierarchy of authority to which a woman or the Church is subject. Similarly the Church, the bride of Christ, has three heads – God, Christ, and the Pope.

The spyryte of every naturall body gyveth lyfe noo forther, but to the members & partes of the same body, which be naturally joyned unto the heed. And so lykewyse it must be in the mystycall body of our mother holy chirche. For asmoche than as this wretched man [Luther] hath devyded hymselfe from the heed of this body, whiche is the vycare of chryste, how can he have in hym the spyryte of this body whiche is the spyryte of trouthe.[6]

Even King Henry, the amateur theologian, rallied to assert the seven sacraments and protect his subjects from Luther's attempt "to enfect you with the deedly corruption and contagious odour of his pestylent errours".[7]

Although there was a steady trickle of Lutheran literature into England, the challenge to ecclesiastical authority was first significantly raised by William Tyndale's translation of the New Testament into English (1525). The debate in print between More and Tyndale is the first great controversy of the English Reformation. More's *Dialogue Concerning Tyndale* is perhaps the best defense of the Catholic establishment to be written in English. The writer's purpose is to assert the twin virtues of unity and charity in the Church. Faith in Christ is preserved in the whole church, "the whole congregation of Christian people professing his name and his faith, and abiding in the body of the same, not being precided and cut off, meaning that his faith should never so utterly fail in his church but that it should whole and entire abide and remain therein".[8] Peter, with his successors, is head of the Church.[9] In the "Letter to John Firth" (1532) More concludes a long discussion of the nature of the Eucharist by saying that the bread is a sure sign of salvation, a token "that our soulys by the fayth thereof, and our bodyes by the receyvynge therof, may be spyrytually and bodily joyned and knyt unto hys here in erth, and wyth his holy soule and his blessed body . . . gloryously lyve after in heven".[10] In defining the relationship

---

[6] Fisher, "Sermon Against Luther", *English Works*, p. 322.
[7] Henry VIII, *A copy of the letters wherin . . . Henry the eight . . . made answere unto a certeyn letter of Martyn Luther* (London, n.d.), sig. A6. Henry acknowledges that the estate of a king is inferior to that of the Pope (sig. F2v).
[8] More *Dialogue Concerning Tyndale*, ed. W. E. Campbell (London, 1927), p. 68.
[9] More, *Dialogue Concerning Tyndale*, p. 68; see also pp. 118, 133, 144.
[10] *The Correspondence of Sir Thomas More*, ed. Elizabeth F. Rogers (Princeton, 1947), p. 463.

of heretics to the church More uses both the analogy of the human body and of vine and its branches.[11] An unauthorized translation of Scripture denies, at least implicitly, the authority of the Church and is therefore heretical. A heretic, who has not been excommunicated ("cut off for fear of corruption"), hangs on the Church by "some little light or life", the spirit of God's grace which upholds the body of the Church and which may yet redeem the "dead hand . . . a burden in the body [rather] than verily any member, organ, or instrument thereof".[12] In the "Letter to Firth" More writes "For as the canker corrupteth the body ferther and ferther, and turneth the hole partes into the same dedely sykeness: so do these heretykes crepe forth among good symple soulys, and . . . dayly wyth suche abomynable bokes corrupte and destroye in corners very many. . . ."[13]

More recognizes the abuses which exist in the Church; he relates the popular legend of St. Uncumber, who frees women from their husbands, and describes those who, like Chaucer's Pardoner, deceive the people with sheep's bones.[14] The heresies of the Lutherans are not the answer, however, for the Lutherans seem to be blind to the inevitable imperfections in any human institution.

But our Lord in this his mystical body of his church, carried his members some sick, some whole, and all sickly. Nor they be not for every sin clean cast off from the body, but if they be for fear of infection cut off, or else willingly do depart and separate themself as do these heretics. . . .[15]

Only in Heaven, after the day of doom, will the Church be purified:

then shall all these scalde and scabbed pieces scale clean off, and the whole body of Christ's holy church remain pure, clean and glorious without wem, wrinkle or spot. . . .[16]

But though the Church on earth is "as scabbed as ever was Job . . . yet her loving spouse leaveth her not, but continually goeth about by many manner medicines, some bitter, some sweet, some easy, some grievous, some pleasant, some painful, to cure her".[17]

In the *Apologye* (1532) More says that reform must begin with a man's looking into his own heart and with an attack on the obviously

---

[11] From John XV. 5,6; More, *Dialogue Concerning Tyndale*, pp. 134, 144. Lutherans are "withering branches".
[12] More, *Dialogue Concerning Tyndale*, pp. 134-35.
[13] More, *Correspondence*, p. 441.
[14] More, *Dialogue Concerning Tyndale*, pp. 161, 61, 153.
[15] More, *Dialogue Concerning Tyndale*, p. 143.
[16] More, *Dialogue Concerning Tyndale*, p. 143.
[17] More, *Dialogue Concerning Tyndale*, p. 143.

wicked – thieves, murderers, and heretics.[18] The clergy and laity, the
soul and body of the commonwealth, ought

eche wyth other lovyngly to accorde and agre and accordynge to the good
auncyent lawes and commendable usages long contynued in this noble
realme, eyther parte endevour them selfe dylygently to represse and kepe
under those evyll and ungracyous folke, that lyke sores, scabbes, and can-
kers, trouble and vexe the body and of all them to cure suche as may be
cured, & for helth of the whole body, cutte and caste of the incurable
cancred partes there fro. . . .[19]

But when the need for a legitimate male heir drove Henry VIII to
divorce Catherine of Aragon and, in the course of events, to become by
act of Parliament "the only Supreme Head in earth of the Church of
England",[20] then the case was altered. England was now open to the
charge of destroying Christian unity. In 1534 More wrote to Cromwell,
"And therefore, sith all Christendom is one corps, I can not perceive
how any membre thereof may withowt the comen assent of the body
departe from the comen hede."[21] For maintaining their opinions More
and Fisher went to the block; and Tyndale's *Bible*, as revised by Cover-
dale, was published in England with the king's approval. The defense
of this revolution was entrusted to a group of pamphleteers, many of
them churchmen and many of them educated as humanists. "Bilious"
Bishop Bale wrote, among other things, plays vilifying the papacy as
usurping the authority of Christ, rather than preserving it. But denunciations aside, Henry's revolution had to be defended in positive terms;
this involved a redefinition of the nature of the Church and of the role
of secular monarchy in matters of religion. The Henrician definition of
the papacy followed some of the ideas of the Conciliarists (indeed, at one
point in the divorce proceedings Henry appealed to a general council)
and there was considerable similarity between English and German

[18]   More, *The Apologye of Syr Thomas More*, ed. Arthur I. Taft, EETS O.S. 18
(London, 1930), p. 58.
[19]   More, *Apologye*, pp. 58-59. The later play *Sir Thomas More* contains these lines
by More as Lord Chancellor:

  [*More.*]   Oh serious square,
  uppon this little borde is dayly scande
  the health and preservation of the land.
  we the Phisitians that effect this good,
  now, by choise diett, annon, by letting blood.

The Book of Sir Thomas More, ed. Walter W. Greg, Malone Society (Oxford, 1911),
p. 39.
[20]   26 Henry VIII, c. 1., *Tudor Constitutional Documents*, ed. Tanner, p. 47.
[21]   More, *Correspondence*, p. 498.

exemplification of the principle *cuius regio, eius religio*, even before
the principle was formally proclaimed. More arguments could be found
or fabricated from the writings of the early Fathers. In all of this
Henry attempted to replace unity with uniformity in the matters of
religion; this change had to be garbed with an appeal to tradition, including the idea of the body politic.[22] Both the desire for uniformity
and the appeal to tradition came, in the long run, to a bad end.

The nature of the redefinition of a body and its head may be exem-
plified by the works of Stephen Gardiner, Bishop of Winchester, and
Thomas Starkey. A Latin edition of Gardiner's *Oration of true obedience (De vera obedientia)* was published by Thomas Berthelet, the
king's printer, in 1535.[23] The book denies the existence of the Church
as a universal body with the Pope as its head; the logical conclusion of
this denial is to make the king his own pope. Gardiner acknowledges
Christ, who is in Heaven, to be the sole head of the Church.[24] But the
Church on earth is many – Anglican, Gallican, Spanish, even Roman.
When Gardiner defines the Church as "that only multitude of people
which beinge united in the profession of Christ is growne in to one
body", he draws a sharp distinction between the community of believers
and the subjects of a king.[25] The duties of the clergy are necessary but
subordinate, functions of government; to some God has assigned pre-
eminence and to others the task of teaching and administering the
sacraments: "but as diverse membres agree in one body so in government they should accorde together and every one goo about his owne
office with charitie."[26] The king, whose power is of God, is the supreme
head of his subjects as members of the realm and of the church.[27] Although they have not cared to assume the title, princes defend the
church as the head maintains and defends the body.[28] The medieval
duality of power expressed in the doctrine of the two swords or in a
division between body and soul is eliminated:

[22] H. Maynard Smith, *Henry VIII and the Reformation* (London, 1948), p. 202.
[23] The Latin text and the 'Rome' translation are edited by Pierre Janelle, *Obedience
in Church and State: Three Political Tracts* by Stephen Gardiner (Cambridge, 1930),
pp. 67-171. For Gardiner's doctrinal conservatism see J. A. Muller, *Stephen Gardiner and the Tudor Reaction* (London, 1926); and Shakespeare, *Henry VIII*,
V.iii.24-31.
[24] Gardiner, *Oration*, p. 115.
[25] Gardiner, *Oration*, p. 93.
[26] Gardiner, *Oration*, p. 103.
[27] Gardiner, *Oration*, p. 95.
[28] Gardiner, *Oration*, p. 119.

the prince is the hole Prince of all the people and not of parte: and that
same body of the people ... called the churche is not one handed nor cut
of by the stumpe but that it consisteth perfitly hole the same prince being
as the headde: whose office is to take charge not only of humayne maters
but muche more of divine maters. ... .[29]

This application of the organic analogy allows us to understand Gardiner's comment on the execution of Bishop Fisher: "The churche is
heyled, and nott woundyd, by the deth of a trayter."[30]

Essentially similar views are expressed by Thomas Starkey in *An
Exhortation to the people instructing them to Unitie and Obedience*
(*c.* 1540) and in his correspondence with Reginald Pole. In 1535
Starkey tried, unsuccessfully, to persuade Pole to support the royal
position on the divorce. Starkey combines some vague arguments from
Church history with a Machiavellian view that "The breaking therefore
of order is but a politic matter; like as the institution of the same was
at the beginning."[31] Papal supremacy has evolved as something "convenyent to the conversation of the chrystyan unyte, but in no case to
be of such necessyte, that, wythout the same, chrystyan myndys may
not attayn to theyr salvatyon nor kepe the spiritual unyte. ... ."[32] The
recently executed monks of the Charterhouse thought that papal supremacy was instituted by Christ; but their superstitious minds could
not distinguish between spiritual and political unity.[33] In a later letter,
Starkey cites St. Paul to establish that Christ is the only head of the
church, in which there can be many "cyvle & polytyke hedys".[34] To
extend papal supremacy, which is only tolerated in the west, throughout the whole world would be "an extreme folly".[35] Writing after the
publication of Pole's book, Starkey says, "because we are slypped from
the obedience of rome, you juge us to be separate from the unyte of the
church, & to be no membres of the catholyke body. ... ."[36] But true

[29]   Gardiner, *Oration*, p. 117.
[30]   Gardiner, *Si sedes illa* (1535?), a manuscript tract edited by Janelle, *Obedience
in Church and State*, p. 31.
[31]   Printed in John Strype, *Ecclesiastical Memorials*, 7 vols. (London, 1816), VI, 40.
[32]   *Starkey's Life and Letters*, ed. S. J. Herrtage, EETS, E. S. 32 (London, 1878), p.
xix.
[33]   Starkey, *Life and Letters*, p. xx.
[34]   Starkey, *Life and Letters*, p. xxix.
[35]   Strype, *Ecclesiastical Memorials*, VI, 40.
[36]   Starkey, *Life and Letters*, p. xxxvi. See also Pole's letter to Tunstall saying that
the king's doctrinal agreement with Rome is futile, "except he agree in the head of
the church, that the rest of the church doth follow; wherby *ecclesia* is *una*". Strype,
Ecclesiastical Memorials, VI, 64.

Christian unity is found in faith and the love and charity which knits men's hearts together.

The *Exhortation to Unitie and Obedience* denies papal supremacy as part of an attempt to impress Englishmen with the necessity of uniformity of belief within the realm and of obedience to the king in all things. If "discord and diversitie of opinion" are put away, "if we as membres of one body, rune all together after one fashion . . . it shall minister a great occasion to the setting forthe of Christis trewe religion".[37] Starkey repeats his distinction between the spiritual body, whose head is Christ, and the civil bodies, which are national; it is convenient to have one head (prince or bishop) in a particular region, but it is "playne folly" to have one Pope or Emperor for all mankind.[38] Even as the same diet will not produce good health in all men, so one should not insist on identical religious practices in all nations.[39] If Peter had been head of the Church, asks Starkey, would not Paul have mentioned the fact?[40] On the other hand, the lack of a strong ruler in Germany is largely responsible for the political and religious dissension in that land.[41] Throughout the *Exhortation* Starkey repeatedly speaks of the body of which we are all members, joined with love and charity to one another and to the head, who is variously Christ or the king. But Starkey is almost deliberately vague about the details of the body of the realm; he does not spell out in detail the nature of the relationship between king and church in England and does not go to the extremes of Gardiner's caesaropapism. Such analogies as may exist between the spiritual and political bodies are left unexplored. As in much of Henry's propaganda, the emphasis is on the practical fact of the royal supremacy rather than a precise theoretical justification of it.[42]

Starkey's *Exhortation to Unitie and Obedience* is one example of the mass of literature condemning rebellion or the support of foreign invasion which appeared between 1530 and 1550. There was much to fear. At times it was possible that the Catholic princes, perhaps led by Francis I, might launch an armada; the Papacy supported such schemes

---

[37] Starkey, *Exhortation to Unitie and Obedience* (London, n.d.), sigs. a3, A4. The *Exhortation* is analyzed in detail by W. Gordon Zeeveld, *Foundations of Tudor Policy* (Cambridge, Mass., 1948), pp. 145-56, who considers it the basis of the Anglican *via media*.

[38] Starkey, *Exhortation*, sigs. R4v, S3r-v.

[39] Starkey, *Exhortation*, sig. G4.

[40] Starkey, *Exhortation*, sig. Q1v.

[41] Starkey, *Exhortation*, sig. H4v.

[42] Franklin LeV. Baumer, *The Early Tudor Theory of Kingship* (New Haven, 1940), p. 28.

at least to the extent of drawing up bulls depriving Henry of his throne. At home religious and economic discontent made rebellion and the threat of rebellion ever-present realities. On one occasion the northern clergy declared that "we think the kings highnes, or any temporal man, may not be supreme head of the church by the lawes of God, to have or exercise any power or jurisdiction in the same".[43] The Pilgrimage of Grace was only the largest of a series of reactions to Henry's policies.

Central to the pamphlets supporting the monarchy is the doctrine of passive obedience.[44] Because a ruler's power is ordained of God, rulers must be obeyed in all their commands, even those which are unjust or which are contrary to the commandments of Scripture. The principle of Roman law, *quod principi placuit legis habet vigorem*, was, unofficially, the rule in England; it so happened that what pleased the prince also pleased those classes who were represented in Parliament, so that the legality if not the justice of Henry's actions was firmly established. This was not a little helped by the maxim *Ire principis mors est*.[45] The principle of passive obedience was stated with more rigor and more specific application in the early sixteenth century than it had been before. Because the secular princes were the only possible means for effecting a reformation of the Church, the reformers in England, Germany, and elsewhere strongly supported an increasingly absolute royal authority. Typical of this is Luther's statement, "I would rather suffer a prince doing wrong than a people doing right." [46] Ironically, although the political doctrines of the Lutherans and the Tudors were similar, in England Lutheranism was often associated with the peasant's rebellions which Luther himself strongly opposed. The doctrine of passive obedience is not a theory of the divine right of kings, but is a step in the evolution of that theory.

A typical pamphlet defending the king is Richard Morison's *An Exhortation to styre all Englyshe men to the defence of theyr countreye*. Morison begins by saying that "If men could as well see the danger in a body polytike, as they can in a body naturall, we should lytell nede any

---

[43] Quoted in Strype, *Ecclesiastical Memorials*, VI, 13.
[44] See J. W. Allen, *A History of Political Thought in the Sixteenth Century* (London, 1938), pp. 125-33.
[45] Archbishop Warham at the time of the divorce, quoted by A. F. Pollard, *Henry VIII* (London, 1905), p. 271.
[46] Quoted by Sabine, *A History of Political Theory*, 2nd ed. (New York, 1950), p. 361.

commandement of god, to obeye, serve, and love our rulers."[47] This is followed by a series of examples of patriotic sacrifices culled mostly from Roman history. England is threatened by the Bishop of Rome and his cardinals, who think it "a gay schole poynte ... to breake that lovely bonde, which god hath ordeyned and set in nature, to hold together ... obeysaunce of the membres to the heed of the subjects to theyr soverayne".[48] Chief among these villains is Reginald Pole, "than a perle of his contrey, nowe a foule pocke to it".[49] In the coming battle between the Lion of England and the Roman Eagle, Englishmen should, as loyal members of the political body, be prepared to sacrifice themselves for their country.

The next reign saw a boy king and a protector, a situation seldom conductive to order and security. The doctrine of passive obedience received official sanction in the Homilies of 1547. Homily X, "An exhortation, concernyng good ordere and obedience, to rulers and magistrates", begins with a fine invocation of the divinely established principles of order and degree. Kings are ordained of God and, however wicked they may be, may not be resisted, just as Christ and his disciples suffered at the hands of unjust magistrates. "This is Gods ordinaunce, Gods commandement, & Gods holy will that the whole body of every realme, and al the membres & partes of the same, shal be subject to their hed, their kyng. . . ."[50] Homily VI, "Of Christian Love & Charitie", adds that a seditious person is like a "putrified and festered membre" which a good surgeon amputates "for the love he hath to the whole body".[51] Even such relatively radical preachers as Hugh Latimer were perfectly clear that no subject had a right to resist any command of the king.[52]

Abroad Cardinal Pole was urging Pope Paul III to launch a crusade; Henry II of France dreamed of seizing Boulogne and Calais. In spite of Protector Somerset's moderately enlightened agricultural policy, there were uprisings in the west and in Oxfordshire, culminating in Kett's Rebellion in East Anglia in 1549. The best known of the books answering the rebels is Sir John Cheke's *The hurt of sedicion, howe*

---

[47]   Morison, *An Exhortation* (London, 1539), sig. A3v. Morison's activities as a pamphleteer are discussed by Zeeveld, *Foundations of Tudor Policy*, pp. 174-77.
[48]   Morison, *An Exhortation*, sigs. Biv-B2.
[49]   Morison, *An Exhortation*, sigs. C8v-D1.
[50]   *Certayne Sermons, or Homilies* (London, 1547), sig. S3v.
[51]   *Certayne Sermons, or Homilies*, sigs. L2v-L3.
[52]   Hugh Latimer, "Sermon Preached at Stamford" (1550), in *Sermons*, ed. George E. Corrie, Parker Society, 2 vols. (Cambridge, 1844), I, 300.

grevous it is to a Commune welth. Cheke's humanist training provides
him with a statement that the good health of both an individual and
the state are caused by good government. The twin principles of order
and obedience are defended with considerable use of the organic
analogy. The rebels, like a 'byle in a body", are "the viler parts of the
body", contending against the five wits, the Council.[53] A body, politic
or natural, "cannot bee without much griefe of inflamacion, where any
least part is out of joynt, or not duely set in his owne natural place".[54]
Since the king has restored the purity of the Church, the rebels "have
not so muche amended old sores, as brought in new plages".[55]

Similar sentiments are expressed in Robert Crowley's epigram "Of
Commotionars".

> When the bodye is vexed,
>   through humors corrupted,
> To restore it to helth
>   those humours muste be purged.
>
> Even so doth it fare
>   by the weale publyke,
> Wych chaunceth to be often
>   diseased and sycke,
> Through the mischevouse malice
>   of such men as be
> Desyrouse to breake
>   the publyke unitie.[56]

These humors must be purged by the sword or, that failing, "discrete
counsell", which will strengthen the "humours naturall" so that seditious men can do no harm. The poem ends with a prayer that the time
for the death of the public body has not yet come:

> God graunte that our synne
>   have not broughte us so lowe,
> That we be paste cure:
>   God onelye doeth thys knowe;
> And I truste to se healthe agayne,
>   if the finall ende
> Be not nowe nere at hande;
>   whyche the Lorde shortelye sende.[57]

---

[53]   Sir John Cheke, *The hurt of sedicion* (London, 1549), sig. B4v. This pamphlet
was later reprinted by Holinshed in the *Chronicles*.
[54]   Cheke, *The hurt of sedicion*, sig. E6v.
[55]   Cheke, *The hurt of sedicion*, sig. F3.
[56]   Robert Crowley, *Epigrams* (1550), in *The Select Works of Robert Crowley*, ed.
J. M. Cowper, EETS, E.S. 15 (London, 1872), p. 21. Similar language appears in
Crowley's *The Way to Wealth*, *Select Works*, p. 131.
[57]   Crowley, *Select Works*, p. 23.

In *The Last Trumpet* Crowley sets forth at length the doctrine that a man should obey his king even when commanded to do something forbidden in the gospel.

> And se thou do not him dispyse,
> But aunswere him wyth reverence;
> And though thou mightest, yet in no wyse
> Do thou forget obedience.

> For it is God that appointeth
> Kinges and rulers over the route:
> And with his power he anointeth
> Them for to be obeyed, no doubte.[58]

So far we have examined the idea of a body politic as it was applied to the Church and as it furthered the doctrine of passive obedience. In this perhaps may be found anticipation of some aspects of a challenge to the validity of the organic metaphor. It is one thing for William of Ockham and Marsilius of Padua to discuss whether or not the Pope was head of the Church and quite another for Henry VIII to make himself Pope in England. The Conciliarists do not challenge the unity of Christianity; the Act of Supremacy admits only a carefully defined and limited membership in the body of Christ. The application of the organic analogy to national states which are slowly becoming self-conscious is, of course, appropriate. But the doctrine of passive obedience tends to deny the traditional medieval qualities of love and charity and to deny eventually a king's responsibility for his subjects, replacing natural harmony with force. This was not a problem in sixteenth-century England; the seventeenth was another matter.

There remains, however, one more significant group of writings in early sixteenth-century England which make extensive use of the analogy of the body politic. More than a few writers were aware of a severe economic and social dislocation. Enclosures, inflation of prices, deflation of the currency, rent-racking, and the problems resulting from the appropriation of church property – all received extensive commentary. Although it is now realized that the situation was often oversimplified, the important point is that people were aware that something was seriously wrong.[59] It was widely recognized that economic attitudes were changing. Denunciations of "greed" were frequent. The new capitalists and those enriched with the monastic lands seemed to feel

---

[58] Crowley, *Select Works*, pp. 67, 68.
[59] See general survey by Helen C. White, *Social Criticism in Popular Religious Literature of the Sixteenth Century* (New York, 1944).

less responsibility for their tenants than had the monks and medieval lords. One of the responses to this situation was the ideal of the commonwealth, an appeal to order, peace, charity, and the well-being of all.[60] More's *Utopia*, the first and best known of these works, describes the woes of contemporary England and contrasts these with the land of King Utopus, which is regulated along the lines of Plato's Republic. But More's combination of medievalism and humanism may be consciously an impossible commonwealth, which serves only as a sad commentary on the follies of men.

One of the most frequently voiced complaints was that by enclosing commonlands for pasturage, avaricious landlords were ruining the country: "we are being eaten up by the sheep" was the cry. In sixty years, wrote Clement Armstrong, four or five hundred villages "in the myddell parts of the body of the reame" have been destroyed.[61]

A mervelous sight to see, England for the lakke of the lyvely grace of Godd lyveth like as a beste, which beeng woundyd of the sore greff and smert the members hath sensible felyng, but of the cause thereof they have no descrivyng. So the pore wrechid bestly membris of the body of the reame, every meting with other in company, compleynyth of ther sore greff of nede and necessite of vitalls, clothyng and money.[62]

The cause for this distress is that "No man in England never seketh for no comon weale, but all and every for his singular weals."[63] The reason God established the king as head of the realm is to care for all its members.

What man can say by the office of his mouth, fedyng all the membris in his body, to giff to oon hand more than to another or to oon fynger or to and oon member more than to another, wherby oon to hurt and distroy another, but that alle membris shuld receyve mete togedre to liff out of necessite. . . .[64]

Another tract by Armstrong, *Howe to Reforme the Realme in Settyng Them to Werke and to Restore Tillage* (c. 1535), combines similar use of the organic analogy, some specific information about the workings

---

[60]   J. W. Allen, *Political Thought in the Sixteenth Century*, pp. 134-56. See also Arthur B. Ferguson's articles, "Renaissance Realism in the 'Commonwealth' Literature of Early Tudor England", *Journal of the History of Ideas*, XVI (1955), 287-305, and "The Tudor Commonweal and the Sense of Change", *Journal of British Studies*, III (1963), 11-35.

[61]   Clement Armstrong, *A Treatise Concerninge the Staple and the Commodities of the Realme*, in *Tudor Economic Documents*, ed. R. H. Tawney and Eileen Power, 3 vols. (London, 1924), III, 100.

[62]   Armstrong, *A Treatise Concerninge the Staple*, pp. 100-01.

[63]   Armstrong, *A Treatise Concerninge the Staple*, p. 114.

[64]   Armstrong, *A Treatise Concerninge the Staple*, p. 114.

of the economic system, and several suggestions for improving the balance of trade. He would apply the "salve" to the "sore" of London by having the king suspend the city's charter until foreigners pay for wool with money instead of barter.[65]

STARKEY'S *DIALOGUE BETWEEN POLE AND LUPSET*

Thomas Starkey's *Dialogue Between Cardinal Pole and Thomas Lupset* is, according to J. W. Allen, "by far the most remarkable piece of writing concerned with politics that was produced in England under Henry VIII, with the exception of More's *Utopia*".[66] The *Dialogue* presents a lively and detailed picture of the problems of England and offers a series of sweeping, but practical, proposals for reform. The circumstances of the composition of the *Dialogue* are obscure.[67] It was probably written between October 1535, and June 1536, as part of Starkey's attempt to convince the king that Reginald Pole – humanist, patron of scholars, and kinsman of Henry – would support the royal position on the divorce. Starkey puts words of praise for the king, "so nobul a prynce", into Pole's mouth.[68] But Pole's *Pro unitatis ecclesiasticae defensione* disagreed strongly with royal policies; Starkey's career was ruined and he died two years later.

The *Dialogue* is apparently based on a visit by Pole to Lupset at Oxford in 1529 to try to persuade him to take an active part in politics.[69] Pole, something of a radical and a Platonist does most of the talking, but Lupset, conservative and Aristotelian, has some definite ideas of his own and is not simply a foil for Pole. Students of the lives of both Pole and Lupset feel that Starkey's representation of the two men is not distorted, although it cannot be definitely established that they held all of the opinions attributed to them.[70]

[65] Armstrong, *Howe to Reform the Realme*, in *Tudor Economic Documents*, III, 125.
[66] J. W. Allen, *Political Thought in the Sixteenth Century*, p. 143. The *Dialogue* was edited first by J. M. Cowper, EETS E.S. 12 (London, 1871) and again by Kathleen M. Burton (London, 1948). These quotations are from Cowper's edition.
[67] The best account is given by Fritz Caspari, *Humanism and the Social Order in Tudor England*, pp. 110-12. Allen, *Political Thought in the Sixteenth Century*, p. 143, suggests the dates 1536-38 inclusive; these are unlikely. See also Ferguson, "The Tudor Commonweal and the Sense of Change", pp. 18-26.
[68] Starkey, *Dialogue*, p. 25.
[69] Caspari, *Humanism and the Social Order in Tudor England*, p. 112.
[70] John A. Gee, *The Life and Works of Thomas Lupset* (New Haven, 1928), p. 155; Wilhelm Schenk, *Reginald Pole: Cardinal of England* (London, 1950), p. 36.

Unlike More's *Utopia*, Starkey's work is directed toward specific solutions for specifically English problems. By locating Utopia on a faraway island, More denied the possibility of ever realizing this ideal in the harsh world. Starkey also imagines a better kingdom, but it is in the past: ". . . yf you loke to the cytes and townys throughout thys reame, you schal fynd that in tyme past they have byn much bettur inhabyted, and much more replenyschyd wyth pepul then they be now. . . ."[71] But Starkey feels that the golden age can be revived, if only the proper measures be taken by the government. The Tudor humanists in general felt that they enjoyed an almost unparalleled opportunity to remake the world, or at least the kingdom, by advising the king. The lessons learned from the study of classical antiquity were to be applied to present conditions.

The division of the *Dialogue* is simple and clear. Pole says that

we wyl serche out . . . what ys the veray and true commyn wele . . . the dekey of our commyn wele, wyth al the commyn fautys and mysordurys of the same . . . [and] we wyl devyse of the cause of thys same dekey, and of the remedy and mean to restore the commyn wele agayne.[72]

In each of these divisions Starkey has Pole speak in terms of the body politic and the diseases which afflict it. The organic analogy is important both for the ideas which Pole presents and for providing the structure by which these ideas are set forth. In both substance and form, Starkey's use of the idea of the body politic reveals Renaissance humanism's reshaping for its own purposes a part of the medieval inheritance.

In developing his definition of the "veray and true commyn wele", Pole compares the state to a man:

Fyrst, thys ys certayn, that lyke as in every man ther ys a body and also a soule, in whose floryschyng and prosperouse state bothe togyddur stondyth the wele and felycyte of man; so lyke wyse ther ys in every commynalty, cyty, and countrey, as hyt were, a polytyke body, and another thyng also resemblyng the soule of man, in whose floryschyng both togyddur restyth also the true commyn wele.[73]

That which is good for the individual is good for the state. Three things specifically are needed for the well being of both the body of the individual and the body politic – health, strength, and beauty.[74] The emphasis on "beuty" is something unusual: "yf hyt be deformyd, yf the

71 Starkey, *Dialogue*, p. 72; see also p. 74.
72 Starkey, *Dialogue*, pp. 25-26.
73 Starkey, *Dialogue*, p. 45.
74 Starkey, *Dialogue*, pp. 34, 46.

partys be not proporcyonabul, one agreyng to another, according to the ordur of nature, they be not acceptabul nor plesaunt. . . ."[75] Schenk comments, "It is interesting to see how easily the Hellenic idea of proportion and beauty, revived by the Renaissance, could combine with the Christian teaching of membership in the body of Christ".[76] Pole further defines the body of a state as "the multytude of pepul" and the soul as "laws wel admynystryd by gud offycerys".[77] Lupset quietly observes, "Thys symylytud lykyth me wel."[78] While expanding on the three requirements for well being, Pole equates certain parts of the body with specific classes: the king or ruler is the heart; his officers are the eyes and ears: craftsmen and warriors are the hands; and the ploughmen are the feet.[79] There is no mention of the clergy. This four-fold division of society soon fuses into a simple distinction between rulers and ruled.

The Tudor humanists paid a good deal of attention to medicine. Linacre translated four of Galen's works into Latin. Lupset and several other members of Pole's household at Padua worked on the Aldine edition of the Greek text of Galen (1525).[80] Sir Thomas Elyot's *The Castel of Helth* went through fourteen editions in the sixteenth century. The *Dialogue Between Pole and Lupset* is the most formally 'medical' of all the works this author has read which use the metaphor of the body politic. Discussion of problems and the solution of these problems follows a structural division between body (society) and soul (laws). While the analysis of the soul of the body politic is not divided into smaller categories, Starkey diagnoses the sickness of the body in terms of specific diseases.

Pole finds eight diseases afflicting the English body politic. Four are listed under 'health', one under 'strength', one under 'beauty', and one each for the head and hands-feet. There is, perhaps inevitably, some overlapping of categories. The diseases of health are:

(1) "consumptyon": " a gret sklendurnes" caused by England's loss of population.[81] "When the body ys brought to a gret sklendurnes, ther ys lake of powar and strength . . . so in a cuntrey, cyty, or towne, wher ther ys lake of pepul, ther wantyth powar to maynteyne the floryshyng

75 Starkey, *Dialogue*, p. 35.
76 Schenk, *Reginald Pole*, pp. 41-42.
77 Starkey, *Dialogue*, pp. 45-46.
78 Starkey, *Dialogue*, p. 46.
79 Starkey, *Dialogue*, pp. 48-49.
80 Zeeveld, *The Foundations of Tudor Policy*, p. 155.
81 Starkey, *Dialogue*, p. 76.

state of the polytyke body. . . ." Loss of population in war caused the decline of Egypt, Asia, and Greece; the same may happen in England.

(2) Dropsy: a great number of idle or ill-occupied people, the "idul route" in the homes of noblemen and many of the higher and lower clergy. These are the servants and retainers who make no useful contribution to the common welfare. These yeomen neglect the practice of arms and so in time of need England must turn to the ploughmen to defend her. Pole estimates that a third of the people in England live like drone bees. "In a dropcy the body ys unweldy, unlusty, and slo, no thyng quyke to move, nother apte nor mete to any maner of exercyse, but solne wyth yl humorys . . . so ys a commynalty. . . ."[82]

(3) Palsy: the making and procuring things for the vain pleasures of others – ornaments, fashions, "new fangulyed thyngys".[83] This is directly related to the "dropsy"; those merchants and others who import strange meats and wines, fashion vain jewelry, compose songs, and the like are not idle, but their activity is useless: "some partys be ever movyng and schakyng and lyke as they were besy and occupyd therwyth, but to no profyt nor plesure of the body. . . ."[84]

(4) Pestilence: the want of agreement between the parts of the body – commons against ruler, temporality against spirituality, etc. "A pestylens . . . destroyeth a grete nombur of the pepul wythout regard of any person had, or degre."[85] The diseases of strength and beauty – weakness and lack of proper proportion regarding the number of servants, priests, lawyers, etc. – are essentially the same as 'dropsy' and 'palsy'. Frenzy, the disease of the head which neglects its responsibilities, and gout, the disease of idle hands and feet, are treated in less detail because they overlap in part with material already covered.

For these "sorys and dyseasys" Pole has a variety of remedies. Pole's ideal is one in which "thys multytude of pepul and hole commynalty, helthy and so welthy, havyng convenyent abundance of al thyngys necessary for the maytenance therof, may wyth dew honour, reverence, and love, relygyously worschype God . . .; every one also dowyng hys duty to other wyth brotherly love, one lovyng one a nother as membres and partys of one body".[86] To bring these happy conditions to pass, Pole suggests specific things to be done to cure each of the eight dis-

---

[82]   Starkey, *Dialogue*, p. 79.
[83]   Starkey, *Dialogue*, p. 80.
[84]   Starkey, *Dialogue*, p. 82.
[85]   Starkey, *Dialogue*, p. 83.
[86]   Starkey, *Dialogue*, p. 51.

eases of the body politic: a tax on bachelors (derived from Plato) to increase the population, banishment of malcontents, proper education of the young so that the lower classes will follow useful trades and the nobility will not crave vanities, laws to force men to follow only one trade, restrictions on exports and imports, and so on. These are mostly projects which can be established by constructive government action. Starkey is primarily concerned with the economic welfare of the realm; his conception of the body politic is more biological than that of many others. To consider specific measures for the physical health of the body politic is to biologize morals rather than moralize biology.[87]

Starkey's use of medical knowledge recurs when Pole lists the four "complexyons" or humors and says that as a healthy body may have any of these, so may healthy states be found with any of four constitutions. He then lists three – monarchy, aristocracy, and democracy. A fourth is obtained by distinguishing elective and hereditary monarchy. Elective monarchy, which Pole prefers, is likened to the "sanguyn complexyon" which physicians regard as "best for the mayntenance of helthe of the body".[88] This suggests that the other three "complexyons" can be associated with the other three forms of government. It may also be that Starkey intends his eight diseases of the body politic to be divided into groups of four each group corresponding to the four humors. The diseases of the blood are consumption (produced by weak blood) and the loss of bodily strength.[89] With the phlegm might be grouped hereditary monarchy, dropsy, and the disproportion caused by large numbers of idle servants. If we are intended to associate melancholy (black bile) with pestilence and government by the many, we are given an interesting confirmation of Starkey's insistence on the necessity for dividing society into the rulers and the ruled. Pole would allow the law of primogeniture to be preserved to keep the nobility in their currently exalted position and not destroy all class distinctions.[90] But Starkey only suggests this division according to the four humors, and on one occasion Pole says that many wise men have approved a mixed constitution.

Pole's list of the diseases of the soul does not follow any sort of similar categorization, but is nearly as long as the list of the diseases of

---

[87] In this Starkey follows Marsilius of Padua; see Alan Gewirth, *Marsilius of Padua: The Defender of Peace*, Records of Civilization, Sources and Studies No. 46, 2 vols. (New York, 1951), I, 51.
[88] Starkey, *Dialogue*, p. 58.
[89] The *OED* s.v. "consumption" quotes John of Trevisa on this.
[90] Starkey, *Dialogue*, p. 193. See also p. 110.

the body. Although an exception is made for Henry VIII, the top of
this list is an exposition of the inherent dangers of hereditary monarchy:
one who inherits his throne is as likely as not improperly suited for the
task.[91] Moreover, in England a king is, for all practical purposes, above
the law; there is no point in making good laws if the king is free to
make exceptions to them.[92] True liberty lies in obedience to law, not in
the freedom to ignore it, which too often leads to tyranny. This statement leads to an attack on a number of other legally established practices which are unfair or have in them something tyrannical: the law of
primogeniture which does not provide for younger sons, the laws of
wardship, harsh penalties for theft and treason, delays in the courts of
law, the payment of annates, both the celibacy and the privileges of the
clergy, and so on. For these Pole has remedies of all kinds.

   As part of his attack on hereditary monarchy, Pole rejects the idea
that tyrants are established by God: "But thys ys in mannys powar, to
electe and chose hym that ys both wyse and just, and make hym a
prynce, and hym that ys a tyranne so to depose."[93] Tyrants are not
punishments sent by God and can properly be resisted. Pole does not go
into detail or describe the legal machinery by which such deposition
might be effected. The point is, however, that although he has described the diseases of the body politic in great detail, the organic
analogy disappears at this juncture. Starkey was doubtless well aware
of the fact that the doctrine of nonresistance to the king was being
preached in terms of the body politic and did not, therefore, elaborate
on his logically absurd suggestion that if the head of the body became
diseased, it had to be amputated just like any other diseased member.

   Although it owes much to the *Defensor Pacis* of Marsilius of Padua
and, through Marsilius, to Aristotle, the *Dialogue Between Pole and
Lupset* seems to be dominated by Plato. The dialogue form, the rigid
division of labor, the interest in the education of rulers, the almost
Spartan simplicity of the ideal state, and the concept that the well
being of the individual and the state are identical, can be found in the
Republic.[94] Repeatedly Lupset warns Pole that Plato wrote of an im-

---

[91]   Starkey, *Dialogue*, p. 102. The reign of Henry VI would be an excellent example
of what Pole has in mind.
[92]   Starkey, *Dialogue*, p. 103. Starkey's realistic observations differ from the
legalistic points expressed by Fortescue, who praised England for having a constitution under which the king ruled both regally and politically.
[93]   Starkey, *Dialogue*, p. 167.
[94]   Kurt Schroeder, *Platonismus in der englischen Renaissance vor und bei Thomas
Eliot*, Palaestra, LXXXIII (Berlin, 1920), 75-84.

possible commonwealth, "dreme and vayne imygynation", and that Pole should look "to the nature of oure cuntrey, to the maner of our pepul, not wythout respect both of tyme and place".[95] This is not a denial of Plato, but an insistence that his ideas be given specific and practical application. Plato is the "wyse phylosophar" who recognized the futility of good laws without a good ruler to administer them. More important is Starkey's Platonic emphasis on knowledge and virtue (which is not necessarily Christian) as the organizing and justifying principle of the hierarchy of the state.[96]

With its praise of the past and insistence upon hierarchy and unity within the body politic, the *Dialogue Between Pole and Lupset* might seem to be the work of a blind reactionary. The plea for "one lovyng one a nother as membrys and partys of one body" sounds like an attempt to stop an inevitable but incomprehensible process.[97] But this is not at all the case. Starkey's *Dialogue* reveals a considerable and accurate understanding of economic, social, and political problems. When Lupset repeats the often-heard complaint that the enclosing of farm-lands is depopulating the country, Pole defends enclosing by pointing out the importance of the export of wool to England's economy.[98] Indeed, many of Pole's reforms, such as replacing parts of the common law with the civil law, are in fact radical. In spite of the Tudor's concern for the security of their throne and the increasing concentration of power in the hands of the king and his ministers, Pole is aware of the dangers of tyranny and outlines several schemes for limiting royal authority. While Pole's ideas resemble early medieval ideas of elective kingship, his various councils for restricting the king recognize the importance of the "new men", the educated urban classes.[99]

Starkey's use of clinically detailed organic analogies is supported by the fact that during the first half of the sixteenth century the world of nature was still prevalently regarded as a living organism.[100] The humanists' interest in Plato, moreover, tended to reenforce their acceptance of ideas of microcosms. But Starkey's realism points in an-

[95] Starkey, *Dialogue*, p. 26. See also p. 163 where Pole says that England ought to look for a prince, not such as Plato described, but one who will pay attention to the specific problems of the commonwealth.
[96] Caspari, *Humanism and the Social Order in Tudor England*, pp. 114-17.
[97] Starkey, *Dialogue*, p. 51.
[98] Starkey, *Dialogue*, pp. 96-97.
[99] The Council of Ten, for example, is to include two bishops, four lords, and four men learned in the law (Starkey, *Dialogue*, pp. 170, 183).
[100] Collingwood, *The Idea of Nature*, p. 95.

other direction; close empirical observation of the problems of the realm basically contradicts the premises of a consideration of the realm as a macrocosm. Investigating the miseries of England or the diseases of an Englishman regards as essentially irrelevant any correspondence between them or any higher form to which they might imperfectly conform. The philosophic nominalism of Ockham and his followers facilitates the rejection of theories of microcosms and macrocosm.[101] And, in the seventeenth century, this empiricism and utilitarianism combines with a materialistic view which denies the truth of the statement that the commonwealth is a living body.

[101] Ferguson, "Realism in Early Tudor Literature", p. 299. The presence of both Platonic and nominalistic strains in Renaissance thought is recognized by Joseph A. Mazzeo, "Universal Analogy and the Culture of the Renaissance", *Journal of the History of Ideas*, XV (1954), 301-2; Mazzeo states that microcosm-macrocosm analogies were more extensive in the Renaissance than in the Middle Ages because of the revival of Platonism in the Renaissance. For another example of the influence of Plato, see Leland Miles, *John Colet and the Platonic Tradition* (La Salle, Ill., 1954), pp. 151-70.

IV

THE AGE OF ELIZABETH: CHALLENGE

In the first half of the sixteenth century the idea of the body politic expressed the very real problems of the relation of England to the Papacy and of an awareness of acute social and economic distress. The years of Elizabeth, which for our purposes extend through the first Stuart decade, contained a flourishing of the organic analogy. Although the idealistic social criticism of More, Starkey, and Crowley gave way to the fulminations of Stubbs, Marston, and Dekker, most of the variety observed in the preceding chapter continued. Moreover, the analogy of the body politic found its way into the writings of more purely 'literary' men; this was perhaps caused, or at least facilitated, by a period of relative calm between two social, political, and religious upheavals.

But while the organic analogy was being used more widely and more artistically than ever before, the challenges to its validity increased in number and in importance. Not a few passages we shall examine reveal this ferment and uncertainty. The Tudor absolutism has already been mentioned. A clearer challenge was that of the Puritans with their interest in covenant theology, economic individualism, and thorough reformation; the Puritans' continental brethren became increasingly committed to the theory and practice of rebellion. To the second daughter of Henry Tudor these were distant, often unheard rumblings; the second son of James Stuart reaped the whirlwind. The purpose of this chapter is to illustrate the flourishing of the organic analogy, to consider the initial impact of Calvinism, and to analyze five works in which the body politic is the controlling metaphor.

The dramatists, especially Dekker and Shakespeare, turned to organic analogies for many purposes, whether as banter in a comedy:

[*Babulo.*]   . . . boy learne to give every man his due, give the hangman his due for hee's a necessary member.
Boy. Thats true, for he cuts of manie wicked members.

Bab. Hees an excellent barber, he shaves most cleanly.[1]

or as sage counsel in a history play:

> *King.* Then you perceive the body of our kingdom
> How foul it is; and what rank diseases grow,
> And with what danger, near the heart of it.
> *Warwick.* It is but as a body yet distemper'd;
> Which to his former strength may be restor'd;
> With good advice and little medicine.[2]

At the end of Marston's *Histrio-mastix*, Chrisoganus invokes the comparison in an attempt to restore order:

> [*Chris.*] Behold the faire proportion of a man,
> Whome heavens have created so compleate.
> Yet if the arme make warre against the head,
> Or that the heart rebell against the braine,
> This elementall bodie (thus compact,)
> Is but a scattred Chaos of revenge. . . .[3]

These lines concisely bring together the traditions of man composed of parts and of elements, and the Ovidian account of the imposition of order ("faire proportion") on Chaos at the creation. Another statement of proportion appears in Dekker's *The Honest Whore*, Part 2, when Candido explains that the most perfect geometric figures, the circle and the square, represent government and learning: "The perfect'st limbes i'th body of a State: / For without them, all's disproportionate."[4]

Shakespeare used organic analogies more extensively than any other playwright. *Coriolanus*, which examines the idea of a body politic in depth, is discussed at length below. In other plays there is a continuing concern for the proper direction of a state by its ruler. In the early *Titus Andronicus* we find this passage:

> [*Marcus.*] Be *candidatus* then, and put it on,
> And help to set a head on headless Rome.

---

[1] Thomas Dekker, *Patient Grissil* (III.i.4-7), in *The Dramatic Works of Thomas Dekker*, ed. Fredson Bowers, 5 vols. (Cambridge, 1953), I, 241. There is an almost identical description of an 'intelligencer' in Thomas Nashe, *Have with you to Saffron-walden* (1596), in: *The Works of Thomas Nashe*, ed. Ronald B. McKerrow, 5 vols. (London, 1904-10), III, 106.

[2] Shakespeare, *2 Henry IV*, III.i.38-43, in: *The Complete Plays and Poems of William Shakespeare*, ed. William A. Neilson and Charles J. Hill (Cambridge, Mass., 1942).

[3] John Marston, *Histrio-mastix* (vii), in: *The Plays of John Marston*, ed. H. Harvey Wood, 3 vols. (Edinburgh & London, 1934-39), III, 296.

[4] Dekker, *The Honest Whore*, Part 2 (I.iii.56-57), *Dramatic Works*, II, 151. *Cf.* Spenser, *Faerie Queene*, II.ix.22, for a similar passage in the description of the House of Alma; the tradition goes back to Plato's *Timaeus*.

> *Titus.* A better head her glorious body fits
> Than his that shakes for age and feebleness.[5]

One of the first acts of King Henry V is to summon Parliament:

> [*King.*] Now call we our high court of parliament;
> And let us choose such limbs of noble counsel
> That the great body of our state may go
> In equal rank with the best govern'd nation. . . .[6]

Before Henry departs for the wars in France, the Duke of Exeter offers a little advice:

> [*Exe.*] While that the armed hand doth fight abroad,
> Th' advised head defends itself at home;
> For government, though high and low and lower,
> Put into parts, doth keep in one consent,
> Congreeing in a full and natural close,
> Like music.[7]

A famous crux in *Hamlet* is in a speech by Laertes to Ophelia warning her that the prince

> may not, as unvalued persons do,
> Carve for himself, for on his choice depends
> The sanity and health of the whole state;
> And therefore must his choice be circumscrib'd
> Unto the voice and yielding of that body
> Whereof he is the head.[8]

"Sanity" in line 21 is Theobald's emendation of the Second Quarto's "safty" and the First Folio's "sanctity". "Sanity", meaning 'general good health', is preferable both because it fits better metrically and because it makes the organic analogy more explicit and complete. Finally, in *Cymbeline* the King praises Belarius, Guiderius, and Arviragus as "the liver, heart, and brain of Britain, / By whom I grant she lives".[9] But Shakespeare is not the only Elizabethan to use the analogy nor do his plays indicate the diversity of application which the analogy received.

---

5 Shakespeare, *Titus Andronicus*, I.i.185-88; see also V.iii.70.
6 Shakespeare, *2 Henry IV*, V.ii.134-37.
7 Shakespeare, *Henry V*, I.ii.178-83. These lines are followed by the Archbishop of Canterbury's speech about the order in a beehive. The harmony of the strings of a lyre, the human body and soul, the state, and the universe is discussed by Spitzer, *Classical and Christian Ideas of World Harmony*, ed. Anna G. Hatcher (Baltimore, 1963), p. 8 and *passim*.
8 Shakespeare, *Hamlet*, I.iii.19-24. "Something is rotten in the state of Denmark", but most of the imagery of disease in the play is not in explicitly political analogies.
9 Shakespeare, *Cymbeline*, V.v.14-15.

Throughout the period writers began works of political discussion with proclamations of the organic nature of society. James Chillester, for example, wrote that

The auncient Philosophers ... have ben of opinion, that the natural bodie of Man with the offices and duties of the parts therof joyned and united togythers to a common function, do represent the lyvely image and very figure of a good and perfect common wealth. ... For they did perceive and see, that in the body of man ... there be divers partes of divers and sundry actions and motions, differing muche in forme and numbre, which being knit togethers, and consenting in one uniformitie to the common benefite of the whole, do shew in one marvellous forme of a common wealthe, and there can not be imagined a greater concord than is proportioned by the freendly unitie of these divers and contrary members.[10]

The ruler is like the "intellective soul" which controls the body.[11] This identification of ruler and soul shows how complete was the fusion of temporal and spiritual authority under the Tudor monarchs. A more detailed statement appears in Thomas Floyd's *The Picture of a perfit Common wealth:*

A Common wealth is a living body compact of sundry estates and degrees of men: this body is composed of two sorts, namely the soul the worthiest wight, and of the members or parts. The soule is the king or supreme governour, which I so terme, for two considerations: firstly by simile, in respect of his authoritie. ... The second & last reason is in respect of his being & ending, who is no sooner said a king, then a king of some Common wealth, nor no Common wealth can be rightly a common wealth, without a king; so the body is no living body without the soule, nor longer liveth then the soule remaineth.[12]

Writers continued to describe the various ranks of kingdoms as parts of a human body. Barnabe Barnes, the sonneteer and dramatist, offered a fairly ordinary scheme in which the king is the head; counsellors are eyes and ears; the laws, lungs; yeomen, ribs; and so forth.[13] An unusually graphic detail, however, appears in this sentence:

Riches therefore may be properly tearned the blood of peace, that entering the veines or conduits of the liver, which may semblably likened to the Treasurers office, and reflowing thence, benignely disperseth it selfe into

[10]   James Chillester, "Epistle to the Queen" in his translation of Chelidonius Tigurinus, *Of the Institution and first beginning of Christian Princes, and the Originall of Kingdomes* (London, 1571), sig. A2.
[11]   Chillester, sig A2v. See also Chelidonius, sig. F3. The ruler is also likened to the eye, which gives direction to the body (sig. Iv).
[12]   Thomas Floyd, *The Picture of a perfit Common wealth* (London, 1600), sigs. Blr-v. Notice the echo of Elyot (p. 49 above) in the first sentence.
[13]   Barnabe Barnes, *Foure Bookes of Offices* (London, 1606), sigs. E, K3-K4v.

the members of the whole bodie, resembling analogically the Common-wealth, for the generall sustentation and nurriture thereof.[14]

The king's function is that of a physician to purge "the proud, chol-lerick and melancholick humors" of his realm.[15] Barnes employs an unusually large number of words to emphasize that he is using an analogy of comparison.

The *Four Bookes of Offices*, which owes much besides the suggestion of its title to Cicero, is one of many applications of the organic analogy to inculcate the responsibilities of a ruler. Sir Philip Sidney's King Euarchus, in contrast to the false ideas of tyrants, "vertuouslie and wisely acknowledging, that he with his people made all but one politike bodie, whereof himselfe was the head; even so cared for them, as he woulde for his owne limmes: never restrayning their liberty, without it stretched to licenciousnes, nor pulling from them their goods . . .".[16] In Samuel Daniel's *Civil Wars* there are contrasting passages about Richard II:

> *Our Health is from our head*: if that be ill,
> Distemp'red, faint, and weake, all the rest will.

and Henry V:

> Hee as the Chiefe, and all-directing head,
> Did with his subjects, as his members, live;
> And them to goodnesse forced not, but led. . . .[17]

On stage Richard and his "ulcerous" minions were described by Thomas of Woodstock:

> *Woodstock.*   Enough, enough
> Good brother, I have found out the disease:
> When the head aches, the body is not healthful.
> King Richard's wounded with a wanton humour,
> Lulled and secured by flattering sycophants;
> But tis not deadly yet, it may be cured:
> Some vein let blood – where the corruption lies
> And all shall heal again.[18]

14 Barnes, *Foure Bookes of Offices*, sig. Bv; see also sig. K4.
15 Barnes, *Foure Bookes of Offices*, sig. *4; also Glr-v.
16 Philip Sidney, *The Countesse of Pembrokes Arcadia* (1590), *The Complete Works of Sir Philip Sidney*, ed. Albert Feuillerat, 4 vols. (Cambridge, 1912-26), I, 187. For Sidney's political ideas see Talbert, *The Problem of Order*, pp. 89-117.
17 Samuel Daniel, *The Civil Wars* (II, 114; V, 16), ed. Laurence Michel (New Haven, 1958), pp. 128, 181-82. Henry V united the state and dispersed all ill humors. See also V, 57 (p. 192) and VII, 35 (p. 246).
18 *Woodstock: A Moral History*, I.i.142-49, ed. A. P. Rossiter (London, 1946), p. 83. Similarly, Arundel says of Green: "Cut but this ulcer off, thou heal'st the king-dom." *Woodstock*, V.iv.ll.

The action of the play is this letting of blood.

The use of the imagery of disease to portray political and economic disorder is frequent. There is a stanza in Drayton which apostrophizes:

> O cruell discord foode of deadly hate,
> O mortall corsive to a common weale,
> Death-lingring consumption to a state,
> A poysoned sore that never salve could heale:
>   O foule contagion deadly killing fever,
>   Infecting oft, but to be cured never.[19]

As part of his discovery of cony-catching, Robert Greene lamented that the present generation of libertines are like "the Gangrena ... a disease incurable by the censure of the Chirugians" and must by death be cut off from the commonwealth.[20] In quite another context, a Parliamentary debate about monopolies in 1601, we find the following exchange:

> Mr. Martin: "The Principal Commodities of both my Town and Country are ingrossed into the Hands of these Blood-Suckers of the Common-Wealth.
> If a Body, Mr. Speaker, being Let Blood, be left still Languishing without any Remedy, How can the Good Estate of that Body long remain?"
> Sir George Moore: "Her Majesty the Head, the Patentee the Hand, the Subject the Foot. Now, here is our Case; the Head gives Power to the Hand, the Hand Oppresseth the Foot, the Foot Riseth against the Head."[21]

The same year an unfavorable balance of trade and subsequent drain of money caused Gerrard De Malynes to publish a book with the title: *A treatise of the Canker of England's Common wealh. Devided into three parts: Wherein the Author, imitating the rule of good Phisitions, First, declareth the disease; Secondarily, sheweth the efficient cause thereof; Lastly, a remedy for the same.*[22]

While enumerating "The Seven Deadly Sinnes of London", Dekker exclaims, "But alas! if these were the sorest diseases (*Thou noblest City of the now-noblest Nation*) that Idlenes does infect thee with: Thou hast Phisick sufficient in thy selfe, to purge thy bodie of them"; but the physicians (magistrates) are themselves idle.[23] Among the corruptions in the body of London is cruelty, the Spanish disease (like the

---

[19]   Michael Drayton, *Peirs Gaveston*, 11. 733-38, *The Works of Michael Drayton*, ed. J. William Hebel, 5 vols. (Oxford, 1931-41), I, 179.
[20]   Robert Greene, *The Second Part of Conny-Catching* (1592), ed. G. B. Harrison (London, 1923), p. 9.
[21]   Quoted in *Tudor Economic Documents*, ed. Tawney and Power, II, 274-75.
[22]   Excerpts in *Tudor Economic Documents*, ed. Tawney and Power, III, 386-404.
[23]   Thomas Dekker, *The Seven Deadly Sinnes of London*, in *The Non-Dramatic Works*, ed. Alexander B. Grosart, 4 vols. (London, 1885), II, 53.

Inquisition) or the French (like the St. Bartholomew Massacre).[24] Dekker defends the usefulness of such pamphlets as *Lanthorne and Candle-light* in these terms: "this lancing of the pestilent sores of a Kingdome . . . cannot by any Judicial rules of phisicke, endanger the Bodie of the Common-wealth, or make it feeble, but rather restore those parts to perfect strength, which by disorder have been diseased."[25] Dekker's idea about the importance of justice is found elsewhere, for example in Daniel's "To Sir Thomas Egerton":

> . . . whenas Justice shal be ill dispos'd
> It sickens the whole body of the State:
> For if there be a passage once disclose'd
> That Wrong may enter at the selfe-same gate
> Which serves for Right, cladde in a coate of Law,
> What violent distempers may it draw?[26]

The obligations of subjects were continually stressed, sometimes facetiously. One of Dekker's stage characters says of a salt tax:

> [*Barterville.*] Me thinkes tis fit a subject should
>   not eate
> But that his Prince from every dish of meate
> Should receive nourishment: for (being the head)
> Why should he pine, when all the body is fed?
> Besides, it makes us more to awe a King,
> When at each bit we are forc'd to thinke on him.[27]

More seriously, John Shute dedicates the first English work on architecture to the Queen by saying that as the members of a body perform their natural function to achieve "an healthful hermonye", so all men should labor for the profit of their country, as he himself has done:

And because all the members of the body have chefly and principally a duetie to the head, as governour of the whole . . . So my duety inforseth me most soveraigne lady (the perfect & natural head next unto God of this our common weale), to show a token of the same unto your highnes. . . .[28]

---

[24] Dekker, *Non-Dramatic Works*, II, 75.

[25] Dekker, *Non-Dramatic Works*, III, 179.

[26] Samuel Daniel, "To Sir Thomas Egerton", 11. 151-56, *Poems and "A Defence of Ryme"*, ed. Arthur C. Sprague (Cambridge, Mass., 1930), p. 105.

[27] Dekker, *If This Be Not a Good Play*, II.ii.48-53, *Dramatic Works*, III, 153.

[28] John Shute, *The First and Chief Groundes of Architecture*, ed. Lawrence Weaver (London, 1912), p. 27. Shute's book relies heavily on Vitruvius, who had described orders of columns in terms of the proportions of the human body. Renaissance application of organic analogies to architecture extended to city planning; Francesco di Giorgio wrote that the parts of a city must be proportioned and related "just as the members of the human body". (Quoted by R. Wittkower, "The Arts in

A similar sense of duty led Sir Philip Sidney to write to the Queen warning her of the dangers of a French marriage; in both natural and politic bodies sudden changes are dangerous: "in this body politick wherof you are the onely head, it is so much the more as ther ar more humours to receave a hurtfull impression."[29] The Duke of Anjou would provide leadership for all the "evil affected limmes" – Catholic trouble-makers – in the realm.[30] These are representative statements. The affection of Englishmen for their ruler gave the realm a strength and unity which was its most effective defence. What many had preached was here practiced.

This is not to say that rebellion and invasion were not both potential and real dangers; the Northern Rebellion in 1569, the plots around Mary Stuart, the Armada, and finally the pathetic escapade of the Earl of Essex show that there was much for concern.[31] In 1570 the bull *Regnans in Excelsis* declared Elizabeth to be excommunicate and "cut off from the unity of the Body of Christ".[32] As a result there was a steady production of writings denouncing the horrors of unnatural rebellion and inculcating the virtues of passive obedience. The *Homilie agaynst disobedience and wylful rebellion*, issued as a separate tract in 1570, is the most impressive official statement of these doctrines. Rulers good and bad are established by God; to challenge these rulers is to challenge His authority. The history of England shows that such rebels always fail. The *Homilie* draws most of its *exempla* from Scriptural narratives such as the stories of Saul and David, and Solomon and Absalom; there is, however, incidental use of the organic analogy in the statement that a subject's judging his ruler is "as though the foote must judge of the head: an enterprise very haynous, and must needes breede rebellion".[33] Moreover, rebellion is "an unfit and unholsome medicine to refourme anye small lackes in a prince, or to cure anye litle greefs in government, such lowd remedies beyng farre worse then anye other maladies and disorders that can be in the body of a com-

---

Western Europe: Italy", *The Renaissance: 1493-1520*, ed. G. R. Potter, New Cambridge Modern History I (Cambridge, 1957), p. 132.
[29] Philip Sidney, "A Discourse . . . to the Queenes Majesty", *Complete Works*, III, 52.
[30] Sidney, "Discourse", *Complete Works*, III, 54.
[31] For a general survey of Elizabethan attitudes see Philip Styles, "The Commonwealth", *Shakespeare Survey*, XVII (1964), 103-19.
[32] *Regnans in Excelsis* in: *Tudor Constitutional Documents: A.D. 1485-1603*, ed. J. R. Tanner (Cambridge, 1922) p. 145.
[33] *An Homilie agaynst disobedience and wylful rebellion* (London, 1570), sig. B1.

mon wealth".[34] These sentiments were repeated endlessly from Elizabethan pulpits. In a sermon of the Lord's Supper, Thomas Cartwright, who was expelled from his Cambridge professorship for his Puritan statements, took occasion to "condemn the ambitions of men which will thrust themselves into other men's callings, and take upon themselves, and to be as it were eye, and ear, and hand and all . . .".[35]

In *A Murmurer* (1607) Nicholas Breton denounced the "idle humors" of those who are not content with their station in life; their murmuring "breeds a cureles wound" in the souls of the individuals and of the realm.[36] The structure of the kingdom is described in organic terms: the king is the soul, whom all the parts of the body are made to serve.[37] The eye is the Council; the hand is the craftsman; the foot, the laborer. If one part of the body is injured, all the others will come to its aid. Quoting the Scriptural injunction to remove an offending eye or hand, Breton says, "it is better that a few murmurers perish with their murmuring then a whole kingdome perish with their mallice". "But all this while, there is nothing spoken of the head, that must still bee kept on. . . ." One should not murmur at a wicked king, but pray for his amendment.

Our task now is to consider the impact of the idea of the social contract or covenant on English life and literature. This idea is not of native growth, but crossed from the continent and then found peculiarly English forms of expression and eventual exemplification. Both the idea of the social contract and the idea of the body politic are explanations by analogy of the essential nature of human society. Both analogies – one legal, the other biological – can be and were applied to defend and attack specific political or religious ideas or institutions. The idea of the social contract, however, defines society in terms of its origins, in terms of an original agreement between men or between men and God. It is difficult to use the organic analogy to account for the origins of society; writers who do so usually consider the state to be an

---

[34] *Homilie*, sig. Blv.

[35] Thomas Cartwright, quoted in *The Works of John Whitgift*, ed. John Ayre, 3 vols., Parker Society (Cambridge, 1853), I, 587.

[36] Nicholas Breton, *A Murmurer, The Works in Verse and Prose*, ed. Alexander B. Grosart, 2 vols., Chertsey Worthies Library (Edinburgh, 1875-79), I, xii, 10.

[37] Breton, *A Murmurer, Works*, I, xii, 11. It has been held for some time that Shakespeare's plays dogmatically assert the doctrine of passive obedience, *e.g.* John of Gaunt's speech in *Richard II*, I.ii.37-41 (see Alfred Hart, *Shakespeare and the Homilies* [Melburne, 1934], pp. 9-76). There has been a reaction against this didactic interpretation, for example S. K. Heninger, Jr., "The Sun-King Analogy in *Richard II*", *Shakespeare Quarterly*, XI (1960), 319-27.

amplification of the family, a smaller but equally natural unit of organization. Aristotle is a case in point.[38] But more frequently the order and unity of the bodies natural and political are conceived of as established by God, and the matter is left there.

The history of the idea of the social contract has been capably traced in J. W. Gough's *The Social Contract*.[39] Glaucon in Plato's *Republic* is one of the earliest expounders of the contractual nature of society; Plato and Aristotle were firmly opposed to such notions.[40] Of much greater importance are the covenants found throughout the Old Testament, between God and people and between king and people, on which depend the Israelites' status as the chosen ones. The Lord said to Abraham,

And I will make thee exceeding fruitful, and I will make nations of thee, and kings shall come out of thee.
And I will establish between me and thee and thy seed after thee in their generations for an everlasting covenant to be a God unto thee, and to thy seed after thee.   (Genesis XVII. 6-7)[41]

Gough traces the rather shadowy course of a contract between king and people through the Middle Ages, finding it used by both sides in the Investiture Controversy (*e.g.*, Manegold of Lautenbach), in Thomas Aquinas' thoughts on tyrants, and by the conciliarists. The granting of a fief and Magna Carta are contractual in practice. But until the sixteenth century, contracts and covenants seem to be primarily implicit and inferential, especially in the light of what was to come.

The history of the idea of covenant and contract and its application to the religious and political problems of the sixteenth century is complicated.[42] Of the early reformers, Luther made no use of covenant theology and only briefly flirted with the idea of a social contract.[43] These ideas were prevalent, however, in the cities of the Rhineland before Calvin went to Geneva. Zwingli, Bullinger, and others were

[38]   Aristotle, *Politics* (1252 b), I, 3-4. The family is also the basic unit in Fustel de Coulanges, *The Ancient City* (1864), trans. Willard Small (Garden City, N. Y., 1956).
[39]   J. W. Gough, *The Social Contract*, 2nd ed. (Oxford, 1936).
[40]   Plato, *Republic* (358E-359B), I, 113-15; Gough, *Social Contract*, p. 14.
[41]   See also Joshua XXIV. 24-25; 2 Samuel V. 3; 2 Kings XI. 17, XXIII. 1-3; and Gough, *Social Contract*, pp. 26-27.
[42]   Sabine, *History of Political Theory*, pp. 362-85; Allen, *Political Thought in the Sixteenth Century*, pp. 15-120; R. H. Murray, *The Political Consequences of the Reformation* (London, 1926), pp. 80-128, 169-211.
[43]   Leonard J. Trinterud, "The Origins of Puritanism", *Church History*, XX (1951), 40.

more committed to the idea of a covenant than was Calvin.[44] More-over, these men were directly influential in England through their contacts with the most important Marian exiles – Grindal, Jewel, Foxe, and so on – who did not go to Geneva.[45] The organization of English churches in such cities as Frankfort was a putting into practice of covenant theology.[46] Although covenant theology is not a basic element of Calvin's theology, his ideas are not much different from those of his contemporaries and he was the most influential single continental reformer in England.[47]

The Old Testament covenant promised man grace, election, and salvation.[48] Christ's coming is the fulfillment of this covenant.[49] The covenant is an agreement between man and God, in which God considers man's abilities and weaknesses. Only the elect, those whom God has chosen for eternal life, are the true church, the mystical body of Christ: "But all the elect are so united in Christ that as they are dependent on one Head, they also grow together into one body, being joined and knit together as are the limbs of a body."[50] Doctrine is the soul of the church; its sinews are discipline to remove "such foul and decaying members" as are a disgrace to the head.[51] The headship of the church is not transferable to the Pope; it is the duty of the true church, the elect, to remove themselves from the false church of Rome.[52]

These are relatively minor elements in Calvin's thought, but elements which were capable of great expansion. The same is true of Calvin's ideas about political obedience. His exaltation of church above state would have delighted a medieval pope. But Calvin did not in any way diminish the respect and obedience due secular authorities, especially Francis I of France, on whom he had relied to carry out the reformation. "For since the magistrate cannot be resisted without God being

---

[44]   Trinterud, "Origins of Puritanism", p. 38. Zwingli's *De Testamento seu Foedere Dei Unico et Eterno* (1534) is of seminal importance.
[45]   M. H. Knappen, *Tudor Puritanism* (Chicago, 1939), p. 178.
[46]   Trinterud, "Origins of Puritanism", p. 45; Knappen, *Tudor Puritanism*, pp. 149-62.
[47]   Everett H. Emerson, "Calvin and Covenant Theology", *Church History*, XXV (1956), 136, 142; Knappen, *Tudor Puritanism*, p. 135.
[48]   John Calvin, *Institutes of the Christian Religion* (II.x.4), trans. Ford L. Battles, The Library of Christian Classics, 2 vols. (Philadelphia, 1960), I, 431.
[49]   Calvin, *Institutes* (II.x.4), I, 432; (IV.xvi.15), II, 1337.
[50]   Calvin, *Institutes* (IV.i.2), II, 1014.
[51]   Calvin, *Institutes* (IV.xii.1,5), II, 1230, 1232.
[52]   Calvin, *Institutes* (IV.vi.9-10; IV.ii.9-11), II, 1110-11, 1049-51.

resisted at the same time, even though it seems that an unarmed magistrate can be despised with impunity still God is armed to avenge mightily this contempt toward himself."[53] But there were several small exceptions which could, by zealous and endangered Calvinists, be magnified out of all proportion. In a passage added to the *Institutes* in 1559, there is a sentence to the effect that obedience to man must not interfere with obedience to God. Elsewhere Calvin recognizes that in some states there are constitutional officers, such as the Roman tribunes or the Spartan ephors, whose duty is to resist tyrannical rulers.[54] As far as Calvin was concerned, these lesser magistrates existed primarily in the pages of the ancients. But these loopholes were invaluable when Calvinist churches in Scotland and France turned from passive obedience to active resistance against governments which refused to adopt and enforce godly doctrine and discipline.

Faced by a ruler and clergy firmly committed to Rome, John Knox flatly stated the right of rebellion. "If their princes exceed their bounds . . . no doubt that they should be resisted, even by power."[55] In France the most important of the many Huguenot tracts evoked by the Massacre of St. Bartholomew's Day was the *Vindiciae contra tyrannos*, published anonymously in 1579 and reprinted widely all over Europe.[56] The *Vindiciae* turns upon the idea of a twofold contract. A community becomes a church as the result of a covenant between God and the people, including their ruler. The second is a political agreement which establishes the authority of the king and limits it to the service of the whole realm. There is no contradiction in saying that the power of a king comes from one agreement with God and another with his subjects. The king may be lawfully resisted and even overthrown, if he does not uphold the faith of his subjects or acts in such a way as to become a tyrant.

In Elizabethan England there was no need for such radical views; the reformers desired to work within the framework of the established church. Earlier, however, in exile under Mary, Bishop John Ponet wrote a remarkable little book, *A Short Treatise of politike power*. Although

---

[53] Calvin, *Institutes* (IV.xx.23), II, 1511.
[54] Calvin, *Institutes* (IV.xx.31), II, 1519).
[55] John Knox, *The History of the Reformation of Religion in Scotland*, ed. Cuthbert Lennox (London, 1905), p. 234.
[56] *Vindiciae contra tyrannos*, ed. H. J. Laski (London, 1924). See Sabine, *History of Political Theory*, pp. 377-84; Allen, *Political Thought in the Sixteenth Century*, pp. 314-31; Gough, *Social Contract*, pp. 52-55. Many scholars attribute the work to Hubert Languet.

he makes no mention of religion, Ponet clearly has the current situation in mind when he says that "if the sinowes be to muche racked and stretched out, or to muche shrinked together, it brideth wonderfull paines and deformitie in mannes body: so if Obedience be to muche or to litell in a common wealth, it causeth much evil and disorder".[57] Shortly after this occurs the statement that

Common wealthes and realmes may live, whan the head is cut of, and may put on a newe head, that is, make them a newe governour, whan they see their olde head seke to muche his owne will and not the wealthe of the hole body, for the which he was onle ordained.[58]

During Elizabeth's reign the Jesuit Robert Parsons made some very similar remarks:

The Body Natural, if it had the same ability that when it had an aking or sickly Head, it would cut it off and take another. I doubt not but it would so ... rather than all the other parts should perish or live in pain and continual torment.[59]

To argue seriously, as both Ponet and Parsons do, that decapitation is a feasible remedy for a diseased body politic is to wreak havoc upon the metaphor. If the metaphor is valid, then its application in this manner is absurd; the opponents of Parsons, at least, were quick to point this out:

A noble Metaphor indeed, which I thus retort upon himself. For seeing without the Head, the Body is only a dead Carcass, and can do nothing of itself without the Head, which is the seat of all the Animal Senses, therefore the Body can do nothing against the Head, seeing without the body it is dead, neither had it Power over any Member, but with the consent of the Head. Who could endure such a Metaphor, that a Body may cut off its own Head, that it may remain a Body?[60]

In the pamphlet warfare provoked by the Puritan attack on the Elizabethan bishops, both sides had recourse to organic analogies. The Puritans contended that the form of church government had been set forth in the New Testament and that no one, especially a secular ruler, had any right to "maime or deforme the body of Christ, which is the

---

[57] John Ponet, *A Short Treatise of politike power* (Strassburg, 1556), sig. C8. See also Winthrop S. Hudson, *John Ponet: Advocate of Limited Monarchy* (Chicago, 1942), esp. pp. 131-62.
[58] Ponet, *Short Treatise*, sig. D7.
[59] Robert Parsons, *A Conference about the Next Succession to the Crowne of England* (1594), quoted in James E. Phillips, *The State in Shakespeare's Greek and Roman Plays* (New York, 1940), p. 67.
[60] Thomas Craig, *Concerning the Right of Succession to the Kingdom of England*, ed. J. G. (London, 1703), p. 167.

Church . . .".[61] The first half of *Hay any worke for Cooper*, the second of the tracts by Martin Marprelate, is devoted to denying that bishops may be established in the body of the church.

Do you thinke *T. C.* that the majestrat may make an eie for the visible body of the church . . . can he make a foote or a hand for that body? I pray in what place would you have them placed? If our Saviour Christ hath left behind him a perfect body: surely he hath left therein no place or no use for members of the majestrates making & invention. . . .[62]

Bishop Cooper, a choleric member, is perhaps suggesting that the natural eyes and hands be cut off so that wooden ones may be substituted in their place. The Puritan position is summed up in one of the *Theses Martinianae*: "That our church-government in England by lord bishops, and bishops, is a government of maimed, unnaturall, and deformed members, serving for no use in the church of God. . . ."[63]

Martin's blasts drew counterblasts. John Lyly charged that ". . .with your painted conscience [you] have coloured the religion of divers, spreading through the veynes of the Commonwealth like poyson, the doggednes of your devotions; which entring in like the smoothnes of cyle into the flesh, fretteth in time like quicksilver into the bones."[64] Nashe defended the bishops as skillful physicians, able to detect the fever of heresy, and concluded "the readie course to poison her majesties loving people, is to discredite the Phisitions of soules unto them, and to suffer everie *Martin* and Mounte-banke to practise on them".[65] A calmer approach was that of Matthew Sutcliffe, Dean of Exeter, who criticized the Puritan's use of the simile of the members of the body: "for the Church & common wealth being two bodies in divers respects are unfitly compared to one naturall body."[66] Arguing from the comparison makes it impossible for a man to move to higher or lower office in church or state.

Another development, of little real importance in the sixteenth century, was the occasional appearance of congregations who, without

[61] Martin Marprelate, *Hay any worke for Cooper* (n. p. [1589]), sig. B4v.
[62] Marprelate, *Hay any worke for Cooper*, sig. Cl.
[63] Martin Junior, *Theses Martinianae* (n. p. [1589]). sigs. A4v-B1.
[64] John Lyly, *Pappe with an Hatchet* (1589), in: *The Complete Works of John Lyly*, ed. R. Warwick Bond, 3 vols. (Oxford, 1902), III, 407.
[65] Thomas Nashe, *A Countercuffe given to Martin Junior, Works*, I, 62. See also a similar passage in William Barlow (Bishop of Lincoln), *The First of the foure Sermons Preached before the Kings Majestie* (London, 1607), sigs. B1r-v; I Corinthians XII is cited on sig. C1 in defense of the dignity of the bishops.
[66] Matthew Sutcliffe, *A Treatise of Ecclesiastical Discipline* (London, 1590), sig. 01v. See also sig. E4.

tarrying for any, separated themselves from the Church of England to carry on their reformed worship by themselves. Their practice was another step in the fragmentation of Christianity, of the rending of the body of Christ. Robert Browne, the most important early Congregationalist, defined the church as "a companie or number of Christians or beleevers which, by a willing covenant made with their God are under the government of God and Christ, and keep his laws in one holy communion".[67] Two decades later John Downame wrote: "Whosoever therefore are predestinate to salvation, they also are effectuallie called, that is, separate from the world, and ingrafted into the bodie of Christ. . . ."[68]

A more significant response to English Puritanism is Richard Hooker's monumental *Of the Laws of Ecclesiastical Polity*. The work is essentially a microcosm of Elizabethan political thought, for it reveals both the traditions and contradictions which characterized the time. It is a tribute to the greatness of Hooker's book that it reveals the dynamics, the tensions of the age, rather than being a static frieze which embodies only one strand of the conflicting traditions. Specifically, Hooker combines the idea of contract and consent with the ordered and eternal idea of a body politic. The basis for all religious and political order and authority is the law.

Following Aquinas, Hooker defines several types of law. The first is "That law eternal which God himself hath made to himself, and thereby worketh all things whereof he is the cause and author. . . ."[69] The law of nature, "which ordereth natural agents", is an instrument of God's will upon which the maintenance of the whole world depends.[70] In addition, "so likewise another law there is, which toucheth them

[67] Robert Browne, *A Booke which Sheweth the life and manners of all true christians* (Middelburgh, 1582), sig. C3r.
[68] Robert Downame, *The Christian warfare* (1604), cited in William Haller, *The Rise of Puritanism* (New York, 1938), p. 89.
[69] Richard Hooker, *Of the Laws of Ecclesiastical Polity* (Bk. I), in: *The Works of Mr. Richard Hooker*, ed. John Keble, 7th ed., 3 vols. (Oxford, 1888), I, 203, quoting Proverbs VIII. 22. See Sabine, *History of Political Theory*, pp. 437-42; Norman Sykes, "Richard Hooker", in *The Social and Political Ideas of Some Great Thinkers of the Sixteenth and Seventeenth Centuries*, ed. F. J. C. Hearnshaw (London, 1926), pp. 63-89; Ernest W. Talbert, *The Problem of Order* (Chapel Hill, 1962), pp. 41-64; and Philip B. Secor, "Richard Hooker and the Christian Commonwealth" (unpublished dissertation, Duke University, 1959). Although it does not mention Hooker, of great importance for its consideration of the development of natural law and its effect on the idea of a body politic is Otto Gierke, *Natural Law and the Idea of Society*, trans. Ernest Barker, 2 vols. (Cambridge, 1934).
[70] Hooker, *Laws* (Bk. I), I, 205, 207.

[men] as they are sociable parts united into one body; a law which bindeth them each to serve unto other's good, and all to prefer the good of the whole before whatsoever their own particular. . . ."[71] The law of reason, peculiar to man, enables him to perceive his condition and to bring himself into the greatest conformity with God, which is achieved through man's realizing that he is a social animal and that there exists "the Law of a Commonweal, the very soul of a politic body, the parts whereof are by law animated, held together and set on work by such actions, as the common good requireth".[72] This realization leads men to form themselves, by agreement and contract, into bodies politic.

Although government thus derives from the assent of the governed, this assent need not be institutionalized in anything resembling representative democracy; once a polity is established, its laws are eternally binding: "Wherefore as any man's deed past is good as long as himself continueth; so the act of a public society of men done five hundred years sithence standeth as theirs who presently are of the same societies, because corporations are immortal."[73] Although he believes that government without the consent of the governed is tyranny, Hooker's few comments about corrective action or rebellion are very cautious and non-committal.[74] The church is the body of Christ, with Christ as its sole head; Hooker distinguishes, but does not separate, the church as mystical body of the saved, and the visible church to which all men must belong.[75] In contrast to the distinction between church and state made by both Papist and Puritan, Hooker holds that England is a co-operating commonwealth with its religious and secular authority joined as equal members of the body of the realm.

The passages we have thus far examined have, for the most part, been brief and isolated. While enabling us to demonstrate the variety of applications given the likening of bodies natural and politic, these lines from poets and publicists are, at best, sporadic and incidental. In a number of instances, however, the metaphor of the body politic became the dominant image in a work, providing a unifying pattern of idea and exemplification. This is particularly the case in four writings

---

[71]   Hooker, *Laws* (Bk. I), I, 211.
[72]   Hooker, *Laws* (Bk. I), I, 216, 239.
[73]   Hooker, *Laws* (Bk. I), I, 246; man-made law may be repealed by some such institution as Parliament.
[74]   Hooker, *Laws* (Bk. VIII), III, 347-49.
[75]   Hooker, *Laws* (Bk. III), I, 338.

connected in one way or another with the first years of the reign of James – Dekker's pamphlet *The Dead Terme* (1608), Thomas Tomkis' comedy *Lingua* (printed 1607), Edward Forset's tract *A Comparative Discourse of the Bodies Natural and Politique* (1605), and Shakespeare's *Coriolanus* (acted 1607-8). Some of this is coincidence; some, a renewed interest in matters of government caused by the accession of a new monarch; some, the result of specific events – the uproar in the first Parliament, the Gunpowder Plot, or the publication of an English edition of *The Trew Law of Free Monarchies* (1603). The advent of the new produced a final flourish of the old, before king and commons settled down to a long, grim struggle.

Usually a definite distinction can be maintained between personification and the devices of analogy involving microcosm and macrocosm. The latter perceives a series of natural correspondences between two distinct planes of being; the former fuses these planes into an entity which is at least potentially dramatic. Hence the pathetic figure of Respublica in Udall's play is afflicted by the equally personified vices of Misericordia, Avaryce, and Adulation; the order reestablished in the last scene by Nemesis is dramatic, not analogically described in terms of hierarchy or health in the mystical body of the realm.[76] The altercation between the members of the body in the Aesopic fable may attribute some specifically human characteristics to them, but carefully avoids making the body one of the cast. But such a differentiation is not very successful in Dekker's *The Dead Terme*. Formally a dialogue between the cities of London and Westminster, it contains both traditional discussion of the diseases of the commonwealth and description of the two cities which is quite similar to the organic analogies applied to political situations. The distinctive quality of Dekker's pamphlet is its skillful blending of several kinds of rhetorical traditions.

The Dead Terme is mostly Westminster's complaint, partially ironic, about the long vacations between court terms, and London's answer. Mixed with this are several more or less extraneous sections – a list of the royal personages buried at Westminster, a history of London and of St. Paul's Cathedral, an attack on the Bankside stews, and a concluding episode about two London porters at Sturbridge Fair. The result is a vividly detailed portrait showing the double feeling "of glory and distress, of nobility and infamy" characteristic of Dekker's writings

---

[76] *Respublica*, ed. Walter W. Greg. EETS, O.S. 226 (Oxford, 1952).

about London.[77] Dekker's blending of personification and analogy takes place on several levels. There is a small amount of routine talk about the body of the realm: "Vices in a common-wealth are as diseases in a body; if quickly they be not cured, they suddenly kill."[78] Westminster praises the law as providing "cures for these sores of a common-wealth".[79] And it is observed that a fire in a small cottage is a much more easily cured wound than one in St. Paul's.[80]

But there is not much of this. More extensive is the application of organic analogies to the personified cities. London introduces her history by saying that she will anatomize herself – her head and limbs, her birth and bringing up.[81] Elsewhere, the steeples of the 109 London parish churches are the crown on her head.[82] Westminster says that the four sessions of the courts are the four elements which give life to her body. The activity at term time does "stirre uppe my bloud, and keepes mee sound. . . . This Phisick (so long as I take it) preserves my body in health. . . ."[83] In shifting figures, both Charing Cross and the citizens of Westminster are her children, not members of her body, and London is not a part of the realm, but "Grandam almost to thie whole King-dome . . .".[84] The families of the cities are in turn personified. Decaying Charing Cross is Westminster's oldest son, with his limbs broken, his ribs bruised, and his back crooked with age.[85] St. Paul's describes herself organically: there is a head, a body with stone ribs, and the altar is the heart; "yet are some limbes of my venerable bodie abused" by the swarm of jostling humanity looking for business, pleasure, or a dinner with Duke Humphrey.[86]

Dekker's social criticism proceeds in terms of sickness. Westminster complains that the sins of pride, envy, and greed are "knawing (like diseases) at my heart"; these sins, in turn, achieve a degree of personifi-cation.[87] After answering Westminster's complaints and denouncing

[77]   M. T. Jones-Davies, *Un Peintre de la Vie Londonienne: Thomas Dekker*, 2 vols. (Paris, 1958), I, 92.
[78]   Thomas Dekker, *The Dead Terme*, in *Non-Dramatic Works*, ed. Grosart, IV, 53.
[79]   Dekker, *Non-Dramatic Works*, IV, 33.
[80]   Dekker, *Non-Dramatic Works*, IV, 44-45.
[81]   Dekker, *Non-Dramatic Works*, IV, 71. The analogy is then ignored. See also Shakespeare's description of the eyes (gates), waist (walls), and fever of the city of Angiers (*King John*, II.i.215-17, 228).
[82]   Dekker, *Non-Dramatic Works*, IV, 37.
[83]   Dekker, *Non-Dramatic Works*, IV, 27.
[84]   Dekker, *Non-Dramatic Works*, IV, 12, 9.
[85]   Dekker, *Non-Dramatic Works*, IV, 11.
[86]   Dekker, *Non-Dramatic Works*, IV, 46-50.
[87]   Dekker, *Non-Dramatic Works*, IV, 13.

English litigiousness, London makes a speech which, by mentioning the Prince, refers again to a larger political organism:

Thou canst not blame me for opening thy wounds and searching them to the quick, sithence thou seest I spare not mine owne. My pils perhaps may seeme a little bitter in going downe, but in the working thou shalt finde them as comfortable as *Restoratives*.

Take courage therefore to thee, and like a Prince that can commaund his owne affections ... be bold not onely to strike off those sicke and infected parts, about the body of the Weale-publicke ... but also applie thou the same sharp medicines, which I have ministred to thee, if hereafter ... thou perceivest me ready or subject to fall into loathsome diseases.[88]

Throughout *The Dead Terme*, Dekker flexibly applies organic analogies to the kingdom, the two cities, and parts of these cities. These are usually brief and not worked out in consistent detail. Also, in contrast to Starkey's *Dialogue Between Pole and Lupset*, *The Dead Terme* does not enumerate the specific maladies which afflict these several bodies. The result is that Dekker's pamphlet, its livelier style and more detailed portrayal of city life notwithstanding, is less idealistic and less morally committed. The problems are not so grave, not so much in need of radical cures, political or otherwise. There is no urgent appeal to an ideal, healthy commonwealth, no attempt to use traditional political imagery as a vehicle for articulated political ideas.

Most of the talk about the body politic in sixteenth-century English literature was seriously concerned with matters of government, economics, or religion, whether proclaimed in terms of grave morality or given satiric edge. But in the quiet halls of Trinity College, Cambridge, there was acted "a pleasant comedy", Thomas Tomkis' *Lingua or The Combat of the Tongue, and the five Senses for Superiority*. The Prologue announces the play's purpose and plot:

> ... we
> Sad hours and serious to reprieve,
> Have taught severe Philosophy to smile,
> The Senses' rash contentions we compose,
> And give displeas'd ambitious Tounge her due. . . .[89]

The play delightfully combines a spoof of a learned tradition, some

---

[88] Dekker, *Non-Dramatic Works*, IV, 70. See also IV, 38, 54.
[89] *Lingua*, in *Dodsley's Old English Plays*, ed. W. Carew Hazlitt, 4th ed. 15 vols. (London, 1874), IX, 335. Tomkis' authorship was established by F. J. Furnivall, "Sir John Harrington's Shakespeare Quartos", *Notes and Queries*, 7th ser., IX (1890), 382-83. See also H. K. Russell, "Tudor and Stuart Dramatizations of the Doctrines of Natural and Moral Philosophy", *Studies in Philology*, XXXI (1934), 9-13.

satire, and much parody of contemporary writers. The date of *Lingua* is uncertain, but its popularity is evidenced by six editions before the Restoration and translations into German (1613) and Dutch (1648).[90]

Lingua is set in the commonwealth of Microcosm, which is described geographically and organically. The contending Senses are asked to "View but the pleasant coast of Microcosm, / Is't not great pity to be rent with wars?"[91] Overpeering the coast of Microcosm is Mount Cephalon (the head); each of the Senses describes his location on the mountain – Visus is within two houses surrounded by groves on the forehead. Auditus is on the sides, and so on.[92] But Microcosm is at one point reported to be poisoned and at the point of death.[93] Microcosm is ruled by Queen Psyche, who does not appear on stage. Her viceregent is Communis Sensus, dressed in the black velvet cassock of counselors. His aids are Phantastes and Register Memory, with his page Anamnestes (reminder). The principal characters are Lingua (appropriately dressed in a crimson robe), her page Mendacio, and the pentarchy of Senses – Visus, Tactus, Olfactus, Auditus, and Gustus.[94]

Lingua's challenge to the authority of the Senses is in a tradition which includes Giorgio Alione's *Comedia de L'Omo e de soi Cinque Sentimenti* (1521) and a passage previously quoted from Sir John Cheeke's charges against the Norfolk rebels in 1549. Lingua is dissatisfied because her great services are unappreciated; is she not the source of the precious jewels of language:

> The Chaldee wise, th' Arabian physical,
> The Roman eloquent and Tuscan grave,
> The braving Spanish and the smooth-tongu'd French. . . .[95]

She asserts that her mistreatment is due to the faulty information Common Sense receives from the senses: shades of the humanists' complaints about unworthy counselors! Following the story of Paris and the golden apple, Lingua causes the Senses to find a robe and a golden crown inscribed

[90] Hazlitt dates the play before the death of Elizabeth. F. S. Boas suggests 1606 on the basis of some apparent echoes of *Macbeth* (*Modern Language Review*, IV [1909], 518).
[91] *Lingua* (I.x), *Dodsley*, IX, 360.
[92] *Lingua* (III.vi; IV.ii), *Dodsley*, IX, 404, 417.
[93] *Lingua* (II,v), *Dodsley*, IX, 378.
[94] Many of the details are borrowed from Spenser's House of Alma in the *Faerie Queene* II.ix. See Morris P. Tilley, "The Comedy of *Lingua* and the *Faerie Queene*", *Modern Language Notes*, XLII (1927), 150-57.
[95] *Lingua* (I.i), *Dodsley*, IX, 340.

> *He of the five that proves himself the best,*
> *Shall have his temples with this coronet blest.*[96]

Her plan is to have the ensuing conflict resolved by having the crown awarded to her, a curious twist to the denouement of Peele's *Arraignment of Paris*. Part of the third and most of the fourth acts are devoted to the pageantry, sometimes hilarious, of the Senses' presenting their arguments before Common Sense.

But Lingua's scheme comes to a bad end. In the first act Auditus charges that

> . . . you, forsooth, an idle prating dame,
> Would fain increase the number [of Senses], and upstart
> To our high seats, decking your babbling self
> With usurp'd titles of our dignity.[97]

Later the Senses present ten articles charging that

. . . under pretence of profiting the people with translations, she hath most vilely prostituted the hard mysteries of unknown languages to the profane ears of the vulgar. . . .

. . . that she's a witch and exerciseth her tongue in exorcisms.

. . . that she's a common whore, and lets every one lie with her.

. . . that she's a woman in every respect, and for these causes not to be admitted to the dignity of a Sense.[98]

In the end Common Sense determines that in Microcosm there can be no more Senses than elements, but that henceforth women shall have a sixth sense of speaking.[99] After making a distinction between the Senses which serve the soul and those which serve the body, he awards the crown to Visus, the robe to Tactus, and provides a new title of honor for the other three. The fifth act, added as Mendacio says to stretch the comedy out to five acts, is devoted to further troublemaking by Lingua until Microcosm is finally pacified by Somus.

The structure of the play is weak. The last act is largely irrelevant and uninteresting; the main plot is interrupted repeatedly by bickering among the minor characters. But although some of the punning has an undergraduate obviousness about it, much of the play's humor is effec-

---

[96] *Lingua* (I.x), *Dodsley*, IX, 359.
[97] *Lingua* (I.i), *Dodsley*, IX, 339.
[98] *Lingua* (III.v), *Dodsley*, IX, 396-97.
[99] *Lingua* (IV.vii), *Dodsley*, IX, 429. Common Sense lists "the four elements and the pure substance of the heavens".

tive. Old Memory complains about the copious useless knowledge which contemporary critics force him to retain; Olfactus speaks a witty encomium of tobacco. With severe Philosophy smiling thus, there is little explicit political moralizing. It is dangerous, moreover, to attempt to allegorize *Lingua* in terms of current happenings. Nevertheless, it does contain some material which might be found in a conservative pamphlet. The Senses, for example, each have a specific function – 'Visus is a guard, Auditus conveys information, and Tactus compares himself to the hand, the body's soldier.[100] Gustus describes himself in terms akin to Menenius' fable:

> Twice every day do I provision make
> For the sumptuous kitchen of the commonwealth,
> Which, once well-boil'd, is soon distributed
> To all the members, well refreshing them
> With good supply of strength-renewing food.
> Should I neglect this nursing diligence,
> The body of the realm would ruinate. . . .[101]

The underlying assumption of the play is an affirmation of an organically unified state, with each citizen's having a distinct nature and function; Lingua's services, no matter how great, do not justify her upstart ambition to become a Sense. By treating microscosm and macrocosm very consistently, Tomkis emphasizes the rigidly hierarchical nature of society, whereas Dekker's more free-wheeling pamphlet looks at the sins and follies of his countrymen, noting their deviations from his norms of behavior.

Severe Philosophy resumes her thinking cap in Edward Forset's *A Comparative Discourse of the Bodies Natural and Politique.* A landowner, justice of the peace, and minor official – Forset pursued the analogy in more extensive detail than Starkey's *Dialogue*, but for the quite different purpose of claiming nearly unlimited power for the king, or more specifically, glorifying the idea of state sovereignty.[102] Of the "sundry fit resemblance" by which the commonwealth has been described – a house, a beehive, a ship, etc. – the most proper is "the body of man, being the lesser world, even the diminitive and modell of

100 *Lingua* (III.vii; IV.ii;IV.vi), *Dodsley*, IX, 405, 418, 426.
101 *Lingua* (IV.v), *Dodsley*, IX, 424-25.
102 J. W. Allen, *English Political Thought: 1603-1644* (London, 1938), p. 76. See also J. E. Phillips, *The State in Shakespeare's Greek and Roman Plays*, pp. 69-71 and *passim*. Forset's *A Defence of the Right of Kings* (1624) repeats the ideas of his first book but, with one exception (sigs. D3v-D4), avoids extensive use of organic analogues.

that wide extending universall".[103] Forset tries, with only limited success, to keep his analogies from becoming absurd, to avoid "frivolous affection". After listing the four elements of the body politic – nobility, learned men, yeomen, and merchants – he says "How these state-Elements may severally hold similitude, with either the Fire, or the Aire, or the Earth, or the Water, I leave to be conceived and discussed of such as have good leasure to be idle, or like well to be somewhat curious."[104] But he is "somewhat curious" himself, and J. W. Allen's low opinion of Forset's influence is probably right.[105]

Forset begins by quoting "Pithagoras" (really Protagoras) that man is the measure of all things. From this it follows that ". . . as in every man there is both a quickning & ruling soule, and a living and ruled bodie; so in every civill state, there is a directing & commaunding power, & an obeying and subjected allegeance."[106] Forset then argues from the analogy to describe an ideal, and nearly absolute, sovereign. The body may rebel against the soul, but the soul continues to love and care for the body. The soul is chosen by God, not by the body; sovereignty does not derive from the consent of the governed. The ruler is "the derivative, and (as it were) a diminitive of the mightie God" and is not to be judged by his subjects.[107] Forset then proceeds with an analysis of the soul of the body politic, an analysis which has something in common with the land of Microcosm. The understanding is the king's counselors; the "fantasies" are his favorites. The soul's will is the law of the realm, but this is qualified by an awareness of the both sinful and rational nature of man. The humors of the body are the customs of the people which modify or affect the prince's decisions. These humors also cause many of the diseases of the head. The royal courtiers are the body's appetites, and the memory is the records.

This description of the soul of the body politic is followed by a series of maxims for wise government, interspersed with some comments on current events. There is a lively passage about the Gunpowder Plot, which would have beheaded the realm. The cooperation of eyes and hands under the direction of one head leads to a plea for the union of England. After discussing in very general terms the diseases of the body of the realm, Forest advises the magistrates, the physicians, about

---

[103] Edward Forset, *A Comparative Discourse of the Bodies Natural and Politique* (London, 1606), sig. *3.
[104] Forset, *Comparative Discourse*, sig. F3v.
[105] Allen, *English Political Thought*, p. 76.
[106] Forset, *Comparative Discourse*, sig. B2.
[107] Forset, *Comparative Discourse*, sig. D4.

a variety of remedies. Specifically, since it is better to preserve health than to restore it, there is to be no religious toleration.

Although he continually refers to both the authority and responsibility of the sovereign, limitations on his actions are primarily a matter of prudence. Forset leaves it doubtful whether he thinks the king has a right to make law or collect taxes by himself. He does say that it is the duty of the soul to work for the common good, while every part of the body politic should labor for the contentment of the prince – a doctrine the application of which was not likely to find favor in the House of Commons. Both Forset's *Comparative Discourse* and Starkey's *Dialogue* are much influenced by Plato; Forset's sovereign is quite like a philosopher king.[108] Both visualize an ideally harmonious commonwealth using elaborate organic analogies. But while Starkey would reduce the prince's power, Forset exalts it. By concentrating on the faculties of the soul, Forset loses some of Starkey's stylistic vigor as well as diminishing our sense of unity of the whole body.

Before considering the idea of the body politic as it appears in Shakespeare's *Coriolanus*, we should resume our history of the fable of the belly and the rebellious members, for it is Menenius' telling of this fable in the first act that establishes the ideological imagery of the play. The fables of Aesop were quite popular in the sixteenth century; in Latin editions, English translations, and a variety of applications they appeared and reappeared. They were, moreover, regarded as containing "moche morall and politike wisedome".[109] More specifically, in Aesopic collections the fable of the belly inculcates personal morality, friendship, and the love of one's neighbor; the applications in other works are usually explicitly political.

The first printed edition of Aesop in England was William Caxton's translation, printed at Westminster in 1484. Caxton follows the text attributed to Romulus, through the French of Julien Macho (1480), supplemented with the collections of Avianus, Alfonsus, and Poggius the Florentine. Caxton begins "How shalle one do ony good to another the which can doo no good to his owne self. . . ."[110] The revolt of the hands and the feet is fatal, "for the conduits were joyned to gyder". The moral of the story is that "a servaunt ought to serve wel his mayster

108   Allen, *English Political Thought*, p. 83.
109   Thomas Elyot, *The Boke Named the Governour*, ed. Crofts, I, 56.
110   *The Fables of Aesop as first printed by William Caxton*, ed. Joseph Jacobs, 2 vols. (London, 1889), II, 92. See now *Caxton's Aesop*, ed. R.T. Lenaghan (Cambridge, Mass., 1967), p. 117.

to thende that his mayster hold and kepe hym honestly and to receyve and have good reward of hym when his mayster shalle see his feythfulnesse."[111] The fable is illustrated by a woodcut showing the starved body prostrate on the ground, with its ribs very carefully distinguished. The *Short-Title Catalogue* lists eleven editions of Caxton's translation before 1660.

In 1585 William Bullokar published his edition of *Aesops Fablz in tru Ortography*, as part of his attempt to reform English spelling with a phonetic alphabet of forty characters. The fable of the belly appears twice. In the first version, the body perishes through the envy of the members: "A member nedeth a member, a frend nedeth a frend: whaerfor men must uz changable good turnz, nether shall riches nor the tops of dignity, sav a man ynowh."[112] Here Bullokar follows the Latin text of Martin van Dorp in a sixteenth-century edition: "These saied Fablz im-printed by Thomas Marsh iz nerest too this translation that I can ges-of, having lost the book that I chefly folowed in my translation."[113] In the second version, allegedly taken from Pliny, the fainting of the body brings the members back to friendship with the belly: "Great things decay throwh variance: by agreing-toogether they prosper."[114]

There were also four editions of Walter of England's Latin text printed in England in the sixteenth century, beginning with Pynson's in 1502. The fable of the belly is told in sixteen lines of verse, followed by a prose moral, of varying length, about the virtues of friendship. In 1596 a new text was prepared by one Humphrey Roydon. Our fable, the fortieth in his collection, is reduced to six lines of verse and a two-line moral which concludes, "*Nemo sibi satis est*".[115] It should also be mentioned that the fable of the belly gained fresh circulation through the publication of Thomas North's translation of Plutarch's *Lives* (1579) and Philemon Holland's rendering of Livy (1600).

Nonpolitical applications of the fable are sufficiently rare in England so that examples might better be cited from two very dissimilar Frenchmen. Calvin referred twice to Menenius' fable in commenting on I Corinthians XII.[116] Although Christians are members of a political

[111] *Fables*, II, 93.
[112] William Bullokar, *Aesops Fablz in tru Ortography* in: Max Plescow, *Geschichte der Fabeldichtung in England bis zu John Gay* (1726), Palaestra LII (Berlin, 1906), p. 34. See also pp. lvii-lxiv. I do not reproduce Bullokar's alphabet.
[113] Bullokar, *Aesops Fablz*, p. 194.
[114] Bullokar, *Aesops Fablz*, p. 80.
[115] *Fabulae versibus descriptae* (London, 1596), sig. A8.
[116] John Calvin, *A Commentarie upon S. Paules Epistles to the Corinthians*, trans. Thomas Timme (London, 1577), sigs. T3, T4.

body, they are also, and more important, members of the spiritual body of Christ, within which there should be no envy, vain emulation, or ambition, but proper love and respect for one's fellows. In a quite different spirit, Rabelais puts the Aesopic fable into Panurge's praise of borrowing and lending:

... and if, conform to the pattern of this grievous, peevish, and perverse world, which lendeth nothing, you figure and liken the little world, which is man, you will find in him a terrible justling coyle and clutter. The head will not lend the sight of his eyes to guide the feet and hands; the legs will refuse to bear up the body; the hands will leave off working any more for the rest of the members; the heath will be weary of its continual motion for the beating of the pulse, and will no longer lend his assistance; the lungs will withdraw the use of their bellows; the liver will desist from convoying any more blood through the veine for the good of the whole; the bladder will not be indebted to the kidneys, so that the urine thereby will be totally stopped. The brains, in the interim, considering this unnatural course, will fall into a raving dotage, and withhold all feeling from the sinews, and motion from the muscles. Briefly, in such a world without order and array, owing nothing, lending nothing, and borrowing nothing, you would see a more dangerous conspiration than that which Aesop exposed in his Apologue.[117]

More or less political applications are frequent in English writing of the last decades of the century. To demonstrate "that the *Poet* with that same hand of delight, doth draw the mind more effectually then any other Arte doth", Sir Philip Sidney used the story of Nathan and David and the fable told by Menenius, "like a homely and familiar *Poet*".[118] Sidney retells the fable briefly ("for the tale is notorious, and as notorious that is was a tale") and marvels at the speed of its effect on the plebeians. The antiquary William Camden, under "Wise Sayings", paraphrases at more length the fable attributed to Pope Adrian IV by John of Salisbury, but adds that this version is like that of Menenius in Livy, and changes the moral to defend the financial exactions, not of prelates, but of princes who "gather much, yet not so much for them-

---

117   François Rabelais, *The Third Book of Pantagruel*, Ch. III (1546), in *The Complete Works of Doctor François Rabelais*, trans. Thomas Urquhart and Peter Motteux, 2 vols. (London, n.d.), I, 454. This passage and a similar, longer one in Ch. IV (I, 456-58) is the source of a speech about the omnipresence of thievery in Thomas Tomkis' *Albumazar* (1615), ed. Hugh G. Dick, University of California Publications in English, XIII (Berkeley and Los Angeles, 1944), pp. 76, 164. The Aesopic fable is specifically mentioned in Bk. IV.vii (II.447ff). The Abbey Library edition contains an illustration by F. C. Papé which shows how the parts of the body have literally come apart.
118   Sidney, *Defence of Poesie, Complete Works*, III, 21.

selves, as for others . . .".[119] In defence of his use of organic analogies, Edward Forset describes passages from a pagan and a Christian author – Livy about Menenius and St. Paul to the Corinthians. After a brief account of the fable, Forset writes that "the seditious revoulting commons of Rome . . . discerned at the last, that their repining against, and their pining of that belly, whence was distributed unto them their bloud and nourishment, necessarily tended to their owne destruction; and were thereupon reclaymed into their bounds of obedience."[120]

But the most elaborate version of the fable of the belly is in William Averell's *A Mervailous Combat of Contrarieties*, a patriotic exhortation written in the year of the Armada. This short pamphlet contains the revolt of the members in dialogue form; an application of their debate; an exhortation to unity, obedience, and vigilance; and a prayer that England may be delivered from her Spanish and Popish enemies. As in Tomkis' *Lingua*, the Tongue is the trouble-maker in the body. She complains that the Back and the Belly tyranically oppress the other members by forcing them to labor without recognition. Does not the Tongue beg and plead for the body, stir up traitors, slander princes, and induce men to murder and whoredom and all sorts of mischief?[121] The Hand and the Foot make similar pleas and agree to go on strike. The Belly accuses them of unnaturally conspiring to destroy the body. This leads the Belly to give a satiric account of the follies of Englishmen, especially their continually changing fashions of dress and religion. Then, unaccountably, the Back denounces the Belly for gluttony and supports the charge with ample illustration from classical history. Finally the Hand and the Foot feel themselves weakening and confess that they have been misled by the deceitful Tongue, whereupon the Belly nourishes them and all is well again.

The application begins with an affirmation of the order of microcosm and macrocosm: "In this order we know there is a continuall *Sympathie,* no shew of contrarietie. . . ."[122] God has created the universe this way to teach man "what a natural agreement there should be among the fellowships of men, to the making up of a politique bodie, knit together in the unitie of minds." One example is the harmonious music of the

---

[119] William Camden, *Remaines of a Greater Worke Concerning Britaine* (London, 1605), sig. Cc4. Camden also reprints an altercation between the eye and the heart, written in rhyming Latin verse and said to date from the reign of Henry III (sig. c3).
[120] Forset, *Comparative Discourse*, sig. *4.
[121] William Averell, *A Mervailous Combat of Contrarieties* (London, 1588), sig. A1r-v.
[122] Averell, *Mervailous Combat*, sig. D1.

spheres. Another is a comparison between the seven openings of the head and the planets, mercifully restricted to likening the two eyes to the sun and moon, and between the body and the four elements: the breast is the air, the heart is fire, the stomach is the sea, and the legs and feet are the earth which bears up the weight of the rest. These elaborate correspondences show the influence of the Paracelsans, who enjoyed great popularity in the last decades of the century. Extending the system, Averell associates the head with the prince, supreme over all, including the Pope. The heart, the place of wisdom, is the nobility, counselors, and magistrates. The trunk is the middle class and the legs and feet are the "lower and poorer sort". The tongue, the disturber of the body, is the lying Papists who are spreading dissension in the realm. Averall contrasts their disloyalty by quoting the Athenian oath and by lavishly praising the Queen. A distinctive feature of *A Mervailous Combat* is its expansion of the fable into dialogue form, increasing the cast of characters from three to five, and providing an extended and varied, though sometimes overlearned, conflict between the members. Written on a very emergent occasion, Averell's pamphlet lacks the humor of *Lingua*, the vividness of *The Dead Terme*, and the tension of *Coriolanus*, but in its small way anticipates all three.

SHAKESPEARE'S *CORIOLANUS*

As is the case with all of Shakespeare's plays, *Coriolanus* has been the subject of centuries of analysis and commentary which seem to arrive at an appalling variety of conclusions. There is little agreement about a basic method of approach or even about what problems are to be approached. The most common approach, following Aristotle, sees the play as the working out of the fall of a tragic hero. One of the most favorable views of Coriolanus was stated by Barrett Wendell: "The fate of Coriolanus . . . comes from no decadence, no corruption, no vicious weakness, but rather from a passionate excess of inherently noble traits, whose very nobility unfits them for survival in the ignoble world about them."[123] More common is Dowden's view: "The subject of *Coriolanus* is the ruin of a noble life through the sin of pride."[124] Swinburne, Chambers, Van Doren, and Farnham are only a few of the scholars and critics who have followed this approach.

[123] Barrett Wendell, *William Shakespeare* (New York, 1899), p. 330.
[124] Edward Dowden, *Shakespeare: A Critical Study of His Mind and Art* (New York, 1905), p. 282.

The action on the stage, however, leaves one with the feeling that much is being left out if the interpretation of the play hinges on the fall of a noble, but flawed, hero. There is too much in the play that is public and political. One office is established; a candidate for the consulship is defeated and then banished; the city of Rome goes forth to one successful war and then rescues itself from imminent destruction. Much of the impetus of the play comes from the people and their tribunes. In *Coriolanus* there are two climactic moments which define the course of the play – the banishing of Coriolanus and his decision to turn against the city for revenge. Not only must the play as drama present and explain these actions; it must also suggest a judgement on them. Is the banishing of Coriolanus justifiable and, if so, why? Can anything be said in defence of Coriolanus' attack on Rome?

The study of the political problems of the play has brought forth a great mass of criticism which covers a broad range of political opinion. Three categories may be distinguished: those who say Shakespeare supports the plebeians, the patricians, or neither. The smallest group praises the people; Stopford Brooke is almost alone when he says that "the play is the artistic record of the victory of a people unrighteously oppressed, over their oppressor, who is the exaggerated incarnation of the temper of his class."[125] The second strand of opinion follows Coleridge's view that the play displays "the wonderful philosophic impartiality in Shakespeare's politics".[126] This group recognizes that almost no one in the play behaves very honorably and then states that Shakespeare personally favored neither side in the contest of the classes. Gordon Zeeveld says that the play reflects the potentially disordered condition of contemporary England, with particular reference to Parliament's claims to functions like those of the tribunes.[127] A modern variant of this theme is given by O. J. Campbell, who sees the play as a "tragical satire", portraying both sides unfavorably by exaggerating them to look equally foolish.[128]

The third, and largest, group regards Shakespeare as a defender of the upper classes and the fixed social order against a rebellious rabble. Walt Whitman, the arch democrat, called Shakespeare a "singer of

---

[125] Stopford A. Brooke, *On Ten Plays of Shakespeare* (New York, 1905), pp. 226-27.
[126] Samuel T. Coleridge, *Coleridge's Shakespearean Criticism*, ed. Thomas M. Raysor, 2 vols. (London, 1930), I, 89.
[127] Gordon Zeeveld, "*Coriolanus* and Jacobean Politics", *Modern Language Review* LVII (1962), 321-34.
[128] Oscar J. Campbell, *Shakespeare's Satire* (New York, 1943), pp. 198-217.

feudalism".[129] Hazlitt was equally unhappy to find that "the whole dramatic moral of *Coriolanus* is that those who have little shall have less, and those who have much shall take all that the others have left".[130] More conservative scholars have searched for an explanation of what they feel to be Shakespeare's aristocratic political views. This has produced statements that the play reflects the "purely physical repugnance" of Shakespeare's "artistic nerves" to the plebeians, or his reaction to the corn shortage and enclosure riots of 1607, or his contrasting the stability of monarchic England to the anarchy of the Roman Republic.[131]

Coriolanus has meant many things to many people. Because the idea of a body politic, introduced by Menenius' fable of the belly in the first act, was sometimes used to enforce the doctrine of passive obedience, there is no reason to assume automatically that Shakespeare's play is cut from the same bolt of cloth as the "Homily against Disobedience and wilful Rebellion". As a complex work of art, the play places action, characters, and themes in a structure of meaning which is not didactic but rather reflects the political tensions of early Jacobean England by examining the complex problems inherent in the application of Menenius' fable to a specific political situation. When both Coriolanus and the plebeians show themselves to be unnatural members of the body politic, the difference between theory and reality subjects the theory to a penetrating doubt.

Sixteenth-century writers looking for edifying political exempla most often turned to the history of the Roman Empire rather than to the Republic.[132] Nevertheless there was a tradition built up around the story of Coriolanus. The usual opinion was that he was a noble, heroic figure who was destroyed by an ungrateful populace. Lodowick Lloyd, for example, wrote that Coriolanus was one of "the best deserved men in *Rome*",[133] and was banished for his virtue. The contemporary French

[129] Walt Whitman, "Democratic Vistas", in *The Complete Poetry and Prose*, 2 vols. (New York, 1948), II, 243.

[130] William Hazlitt, *The Characters of Shakespeare's Plays* (London, 1907), p. 53.

[131] Georg Brandes, *William Shakespeare: A Critical Study*, 2 vols. (New York, 1898), II, 228; E. C. Pettet, "*Coriolanus* and the Midlands Insurrection of 1607", *Shakespeare Survey*, III (1950), p. 34; John W. Draper, "Political Themes in Shakespeare's Later Plays", *Journal of English and Germanic Philology*, XXXV (1936), 69. The most comprehensive study is Brents Stirling, *The Populace in Shakespeare* (New York, 1949).

[132] T. J. B. Spencer, "Shakespeare and the Elizabethan Romans", *Shakespeare Survey*, X (1957), 30.

[133] Lodowick Lloyd, *The Strategems of Jerusalem* (London, 1602), p. 311. See also his earlier *The Consent of Time* (London, 1590), pp. 496-97.

dramatist Alexandre Hardy saw Coriolanus as a great man who "after many signal services rendered to his country, was at last constrained to yield to the envy of the people, who for his supposed crimes condemned him to perpetual exile".[134] This view was not, of course, unanimous. Thomas Floyd and Bodin, for example, both strongly disapproved of Coriolanus' attack on Rome; for Bodin, Coriolanus was an example of "a wicked and daungerous citisen . . . whom thou oughest to kill . . .".[135]

In the literary tradition, the stories of the banishing of Coriolanus and the popular disturbances which led to the establishment of the tribuneship have little to do with each other. Both are examples of the unrest which followed the expulsion of the Tarquins, but the connection was usually carried no further.[136] Shakespeare's primary source for the story of Coriolanus was Thomas North's translation of Plutarch's *The Lives of the Noble Grecians and Romanes* (1579). Although Shakespeare sometimes follows North almost verbatim, the rather drawn-out and complicated action from the first plebeian secession to the Mons Sacer to the banishment of Coriolanus is substantially compressed and thereby new significance is given to the situation. Three popular disturbances are reduced to one. The fable of the belly and the granting of tribunes are tied to the shortage of corn. The result of these changes is to establish the fable of the belly and its political implications as a frame of reference through which the play is to be understood. The organic imagery which dominates the play maintains the ideological context established in the first scene.[137]

The play begins while the question of the distribution of corn is being debated by the Senate. The mutinous citizens recognize the situation, and their words set the course of the action:

> *1. Cit.* First, you know Caius Marcius is chief enemy to the people.
> *All.* We know't, we know't.

[134] Alexandre Hardy, *La Théâtre d'Alexandre Hardy*, ed. E. Stengel, 5 vols. (Marburg, 1884), II, 56.

[135] Thomas Floyd, *The Picture of a perfit Common wealth* (London, 1600), sig. B4v; Jean Bodin, *The Six Bookes of a Commonweale*, trans. Richard Knolles (London, 1606), p. 431.

[136] None of the Roman historians connected the two events. In Painter's *The Palace of Pleasure* (1566), the plebeian rebellion is not mentioned and the tribuneship is already established (ed. Joseph Jacobs, 3 vols. [London, 1890], I, 29).

[137] The organic imagery is noted by Caroline P. E. Spurgeon, *Shakespeare's Imagery* (Cambridge, 1935), pp. 347-49, and discussed further by J. C. Maxwell, "Animal Imagery in *Coriolanus*", *Modern Language Review*, XLII (1947), pp. 417-21, and Maurice Charney, *Shakespeare's Roman Plays* (Cambridge, Mass., 1961), pp. 142-96.

    1. Cit. Let us kill him, and we'll have corn at our own price.[138]

The Second Citizen, a voice of relative moderation, sums up all of the people's grievances against the Senate:

    2. Cit. Care for us! True, indeed! They ne'er car'd for us yet: suffer us to famish, and their storehouses cramm'd with grain; make edicts for usury, to support usurers; repeal daily any wholesome act established against the rich, and provide more piercing statutes daily, to chain up and restrain the poor. If the wars eat us not up, they will; and there's all the love they bear us.[139]

"The humourous patrician", Menenius Agrippa, takes an ambivalent position on the corn supply. He says that the gods, not the patricians, are responsible for the famine. This "one that hath always lov'd the people" speaks words that have a flavor of patrician ruthlessness:

    [*Men.*]   For your wants
    Your suffering in this dearth, you may as well
    Strike at the heaven with your staves as lift them
    Against the Roman state, whose course will on
    The way it takes, cracking ten thousand curbs
    Of more strong link asunder than can ever
    Appear in your impediment.[140]

    The telling of the fable of the belly is surely the liveliest version we have. Shakespeare's Menenius is more than a little long-winded, which provides the Second Citizen with opportunity for bantering interruptions. As Menenius prepares to relate the belly's answer "to th' discontented members, the mutinous parts", the Second Citizen interjects:

    2. Cit.   Your belly's answer? What?
    The kingly-crowned head, the vigilant eye,
    The counsellor heart, the arm our soldier,
    Our steed the leg, the tongue our trumpeter,
    With other muniments and petty helps
    In this our fabric, if that they —
    Should by the cormorant belly be restrain'd.
    Who is the sink o' th' body, — . . .[141]

By invoking this alternate tradition, the Second Citizen does several things at once. By thus asserting the nobility of the other parts of the body, he both tries to deny the applicability of Menenius' analogy and

[138] *Coriolanus*, I.i.7-11.
[139] *Coriolanus*, I.i.81-89.
[140] *Coriolanus*, I.i.68-74.
[141] *Coriolanus*, I.i.115, 118-23, 125-26. The passage is not in Plutarch. Kenneth Muir suggests the influence of Averell's *A Marvailous Combat of Contrarieties* (*Notes and Queries*, CICVIII [1953], 240).

affirms the anthropomorphic analogy in general as a way to approach social problems. Yet no matter how one handles the details of the analogy, the Second Citizen is "the great toe of this assembly . . . being one o' th' lowest, basest, poorest . . .".[142] Menenius relates the belly's defence of itself and gives the fable application:

> *Men.* The senators of Rome are this good belly,
> And you the mutinous members; for examine
> Their counsels and their cares, digest things rightly
> Touching the weal o' th' common, you shall find
> No public benefit which you receive
> But it proceeds or comes from them to you
> And no way from yourselves.[143]

Usually, when the plebeians were thus instructed in the nature of the body politic, "a perfect reconcilement ensued" and "the cittie . . . againe came to good quiet and unitie".[144] But Menenius does not finish the fable; perhaps seeing Caius Marcius approaching, he says:

> [*Men.*] But make you ready your stiff bats and clubs;
> Rome and her rats are at the point of battle,
> The one side must have bale.[145]

Whereupon Marcius enters with words which continue the organic imagery but hardly reflect a divinely ordered body politic:

> *Mar.* What's the matter, you dissentious rogues,
> That, rubbing the poor itch of your opinion,
> Make yourselves scabs?[146]

After a long speech castigating the plebeians, Marcius tells of the Capitol. Word comes of a Volscian invasion and the city prepares for war.

Marcius' extraordinary military feats at the Volscian city of Corioli earn him the name "Coriolanus", and he is crowned with oak leaves. Then Coriolanus stands for election to the consulship. His accomplishments in battle are recounted at length by the general Cominius:

---

142 *Coriolanus*, I.i.159, 161.
143 *Coriolanus*, I.i.152-58. Menenius' use of the verb "digest" shows how thoroughly the scene is permeated with the language of the body politic, though not all of it is applied for political purposes.
144 Philip Sidney, *The Defence of Poesie, Complete Works*, III, 21; Plutarch, *The Lives of the Noble Grecians and Romanes*, trans. Thomas North, 8 vols. (Stratford-upon-Avon, 1928), II, 178.
145 *Coriolanus*, I.i.165-67.
146 *Coriolanus*, I.i.168-70.

> *Com.*   It is held
> That valour is the chiefest virtue and
> Most dignifies the haver; if it be,
> The man I speak of cannot in the world
> Be singly counterpois'd. At sixteen years.
> When Tarquin made a head for Rome, he fought
> Beyond the mark of others.
>   His pupil age
> Man-ent'red thus, he waxed like a sea,
> And in the brunt of seventeen battles since
> He lurch'd all swords of the garland. For this last
> Before and in Corioli, let me say,
> I cannot speak him home. He stopp'd the fliers,
> And by his rare example made the coward
> Turn terror into sport; as weeds before
> A vessel under sail, so men obey'd
> And fell below his stem.[147]

Even the plebeians recognize the value of his contributions to Rome:

> 6. *Cit.* He has done nobly, and cannot go without any honest man's voice.[148]

They understand that to deny the consulship to Rome' greatest soldier would be highly inappropriate behavior for members of the body politic:

> 3. *Cit.*   ... for
> if he show us his wounds and tell us his deeds, we are to put our tongues into those wounds and speak for them; so, if he tell us his noble deeds, we must also tell him our noble acceptance of them. Ingratitude is monstrous, and for the multitude to be ingrateful were to make a monster of the multitude; of the which we being members, should bring ourselves to be monstrous members.[149]

If Coriolanus were a warrior only, there would be no difficulties – no dissension, no banishment, no civil war. But there is another dimension in the character of Coriolanus which complicates the political problem for Rome and provides the central dilemma of Shakespeare's play. The Fourth Citizen defines the problem concisely:

> 4. *Cit.* You have deserved nobly of your country, and you have not deserved nobly.
> *Cor.* Your enigma?
> 4. *Cit.* You have been a scourge to her enemies, you have been a rod to her friends; you have not indeed loved the common people.[150]

---

[147] *Coriolanus*, II.ii.87-93, 102-11.
[148] *Coriolanus*, II.iii.139-40.
[149] *Coriolanus*, II.iii.5-14.
[150] *Coriolanus*, II.iii.94-99.

The violent hatred which Coriolanus expresses toward the people is a
major aspect of the play. Whenever he is on stage the air is filled with
his curses for the plebeians. These speeches are all Shakespeare's creation and he has put into them the strongest language in the play, for
example:

> *Mar.* He that will give good words to thee will flatter
> Beneath abhorring. What would you have, you curs,
> That like nor peace nor war? The one affrights you,
> The other makes you proud. He that trusts to you,
> Where he should find you lions, finds you hares;
> Where foxes, geese. You are no surer, no,
> Than is the coal of fire upon the ice,
> Or hailstone in the sun.[151]

This is the essence of his fault; in maintaining an absolute cleavage
between patricians and plebeians, he denies the validity of the metaphor
of the body politic. His imagery refuses to accept the common bond
between himself and the people. He calls them animals – "curs",
"hares", "crows", and "geese". They are slaves "To buy and sell with
groats", or Hydra, "the beast/With many heads".[152] Whenever he uses
an image derived from the human body, it is one of disease or corruption – "scabs", "measles", "Boils and plague", and "rotten things".

Because Coriolanus does not love the common people and cannot
comprehend the nature of a body politic, he is unnatural; from his
attitude proceeds the danger to the Roman state.[153] The tribune Brutus
accurately comprehends this:

> *Bru.*   You speak o' th' people
> As if you were a god to punish, not
> A man of their infirmity.[154]

These lines recall the words of Aristotle – "He that is unable to live in
society, or who has no need because he is sufficient for himself, must
be either a beast or a god; he is no part of the state."[155] In a 1598 edition of Aristotle appeared this gloss: "And if by chance there should

---

[151] *Coriolanus*, I.i.171-78. See also I.iv.29-35 and III.i.120-23, and elsewhere. Some
of these speeches are given during battle or in other times of stress, but one seldom
hears anything else from Coriolanus.
[152] *Coriolanus*, III.ii.10; IV. 1-2. The Hydra figure goes back at least to Horace:
"*Belua multorum es capitum*" (*Epistles*, I.i.76).
[153] Irving Ribner, "The Tragedy of *Coriolanus*", *English Studies*, XXXIV (1953),
p. 2.
[154] *Coriolanus*, III.i.80-82.
[155] Aristotle, *Politics* (Bk. 1.2), I, 4-5.

be such a monster extant, which by a particular inclination should shun and avoid Civil societie, Hee ought to be reputed as most wicked, a lover and stirrer up of warres and seditions, and a most bloody and cruel tyrant."[156] The fear that Coriolanus as consul will be a tyrant is one of the most cogent arguments which the tribunes use in urging the people to reject him:

> [*Bru.*] . . . when he had no power,
> But was a petty servant to the state,
> He was your enemy, ever spake against
> Your liberties and the charters that you bear
> I' th' body of the weal; and now, arriving
> A place of potency and sway o' th' state,
> If he should still malignantly remain
> Fast foe to th' *plebeii*, your voices might
> Be curses to yourselves?[157]

Coriolanus does little to refute this view. His political opinions seem to be well expressed when he says:

> [*Cor.*]   I say again,
> In soothing them we nourish 'gainst our Senate
> The cockle of rebellion, insolence, sedition,
> Which we ourselves have plough'd for, sow'd and scatter'd,
> By mingling them with us, the honour'd number,
> Who lack not virtue, no, nor power, but that
> Which they have giv'n to beggars.[158]

This is the problem of the play. The people know that they will be "monstrous members" if they show ingratitude for the services Coriolanus has rendered the state. On the other hand, are they to stand by while a man who is likely to be a "bloody and cruel tyrant" assumes the consulship? This dilemma is brilliantly presented in the brief dialogue between the two officers who lay cushions at the Capitol before Coriolanus stands for the consulship. The First Officer emphasizes Coriolanus' pride and dislike of the people:

> *1. Off.*   . . . but he's vengeance
> proud and loves not the common people.
>   Now, to seem to affect the malice and
> displeasure of the people is as bad as that which he dislikes, to flatter them
> for their love.[159]

---

[156] Cited in F. N. Lees, "*Coriolanus*, Aristotle, and Bacon", *Review of English Studies*, n. s. I (1950), p. 119.
[157] *Coriolanus*, II.iii.185-93.
[158] *Coriolanus*, III.i.68-74.
[159] *Coriolanus*, II.ii.5-6, 23-25.

The Second Officer defends Coriolanus:

2. *Off.* He hath deserved worthily of his country; and his ascent is not by such easy degrees as those who, having been supple and courteous to the people, bonneted, without any further deed to have them at all into their estimation and report.[160]

The dialogue concludes in a line filled with suggestive meaning:

1. *Off.* No more of him; he's a worthy man.[161]

The line sharpens the horns of the dilemma and points the way to the action to follow.

In the Third Act Menenius and the tribunes discuss the problem of Coriolanus using the imagery of the body politic:

> *Sic.* He's a disease that must be cut away.
> *Men.* O, he's a limb that has but a disease;
> Mortal to cut it off; to cure it, easy.
> *Bru.* When he did love his country,
> It honour'd him.
> *Men.* The service of the foot
> Being once gangren'd, is not then respected
> For what it once was, –
> *Bru.* We'll hear no more,
> Pursue him to his house and pluck him thence,
> Lest his infection, being of catching nature,
> Spread further.[162]

Even the patrician Menenius accepts the idea that Coriolanus is a diseased member; the scene reminds us that Coriolanus is both a diseased member of the state and its strongest fighting arm. Urged by their tribunes, the people vote first to throw Coriolanus from the Tarpeian Rock and then soften this sentence to banishment. Coriolanus leaves the city declaring that he banishes it.

Because it is accomplished by established (though manipulated) procedures, the banishing of Coriolanus is not comparable to the Jack Cade rebellion in *Henry VI*, part 2. Nor is it like the removal of such tyrannical rulers as Macbeth or Richard III, which is done without the participation of the lower classes. The banishing of Coriolanus is a unique situation in Shakespeare and it raises complex questions to which he offers no simple answer. Such answers as are given must be found in the last two acts of the play, which are both the result of and a comment on what has preceded.

---

[160] *Coriolanus*, II.ii.26-31.
[161] *Coriolanus*, II.ii.39.
[162] *Coriolanus*, III.i.295-97, 305-11.

With Coriolanus gone, Rome enjoys a temporary peace, which seems to contradict Senatorial prophecies of doom:

> [*Sic.*]   The present peace
> And quietness of the people, which before
> Were in a wild hurry here, do make his friends
> Blush that the world goes well, who rather had,
> Though themselves did suffer by 't, behold
> Dissentious numbers pest'ring streets than see
> Our tradesmen singing in their shops and going
> About their functions friendly.[163]

But this is the quiet before the storm. Coriolanus joins forces with the Volscian general, Aufidius, and leads the Volscian army to a series of victories which threaten Rome. The plebeians begin to repent their ingratitude:

> [*3. Cit.*]   That we did, we did for the best; and though we willingly consented to his banishment, yet it was against our will.[164]

Cominius tells how Coriolanus has become less and less of a natural, political man:

> [*Com.*]   Coriolanus
> He would not answer to; forbade all names;
> He was a kind of nothing, titleless,
> Till he had forg'd himself a name o' th' fire
> Of burning Rome.[165]

In North's Plutarch, Coriolanus' motive was one of vengeance on the lower classes: "For his chiefest purpose was, to increase still the malice and dissention between the nobilitie, and the communaltie: and to drawe that on, he was very carefull to keepe the noble mens landes and goods safe from harme and burning."[166] Shakespeare alters this significantly:

> *Com.*   I offered to awaken his regard
> For 's private friends; his answer to me was,
> He could not stay to pick them in a pile
> Of noisome musty chaff. He said 'twas folly,
> For one poor grain or two, to leave unburnt
> And still to nose th' offence.[167]

---

163   *Coriolanus*, IV.vi.2-9.
164   *Coriolanus*, IV.vi.144-46.
165   *Coriolanus*, V.i.11-14.
166   Plutarch, *Lives*, II, 208.
167   *Coriolanus*, V.i.23-28.

By contrast, in *Timon of Athens* Alcibiades disbands his army after being promised a redress of grievances.

Is Coriolanus' attack on Rome an appropriate punishment for the ungrateful citizens? Or does his behavior prove that the tribunes knew what they were doing when they provoked the people against him? Is the body politic afflicted by rebellious feet or a diseased arm? Can rebellion against tyranny be justified? Shakespeare can resolve these questions only in essentially non-political terms. The most public of Shakespeare's plays becomes for a moment intimately personal as Coriolanus surrenders to the pleas of his mother. He arranges an honorable truce between the Romans and the Volscians; this is the opportunity for the jealous Aufidius to kill him. The conclusion of the play contains multiple ironies. Volumnia, who molded her son's character, destroys him by forcing him to be untrue to himself. The truce, an act of citizenship and membership in the body politic, is an act of suicide. And it is Aufidius, the only man whom Coriolanus considered his equal, who accomplishes the task first proclaimed by the detested plebeians.

In *Coriolanus*, Shakespeare takes the metaphor of the body politic and raises it from the level of political and religious controversy to the higher plane of art. The body politic provides language with which to discuss political acts and an ideal by which to judge them. The tragedy emerges from the breach between the ideal of the "very and true common weal" and the imperfect men who live on this imperfect earth. Coriolanus has about him aspects of the divine and the beastly; the price he must pay for humanity, for citizenship, is his life.

V

LEVIATHAN AT WHITEHALL

It is relatively easy to document the flourishing of a particular pattern of thought; to illustrate decadence is another matter. Moreover, since the comparison of a human body to the state or society never really disappeared from the pages of English writers, it is a process of fossilization, as it were, with which we must cope. But in the first half of the seventeenth century the metaphor of the body politic did lose much of its capacity for conveying political ideas, and to poets and pamphleteers alike it became a much less attractive device of ornamentation or organization. The demonstration of this situation is a three-fold task. There was a marked decline in the quantity and quality of the applications of the organic analogy. But this is largely negative evidence which may be based on insufficient reading. Second, there are a few explicit attacks on the validity of the comparison; these are rare, however; we are more likely to forget than abuse that which we do not need. The third and most important consideration is the nearly complete substitution of the theory of the social contract, the triumph of a science which did not include the idea of microcosms, and the increasing influence of those social and economic classes to whom these 'modern' modes of thought were most congenial and useful. There is much simplification, but perhaps some truth, in a statement that the metaphor of the body politic died with the king at Whitehall.

Francis Bacon has been called the most typical Elizabethan political thinker; this was intended as a compliment, but the opposite may be more accurate.[1] Bacon, however, may be more appropriately considered as one of the first representatives of a later era for two reasons: his unexceptional uses of the organic analogy in the *Essays* appear, for the most part, in the 1625 edition; his materialism and rejection of the Paracelsans destroy the philosophic underpinnings of the validity of the analogy.

[1] Hellmut Bock, *Staat und Gesellschaft bei Francis Bacon* (Berlin, 1937), p. 23.

It is difficult to deal confidently with Bacon's political thinking.[2] His statements are scattered throughout his works and are mostly in the form of traditional aphorisms and practical advice. Like Machiavelli, to whom he refers with approval, Bacon was not so much interested in the nature of society as in the exercise of authority; when he used organic analogies, they exemplify the activities of the ruler rather than the obligations of the citizens or abuses of the system. There are occasional exceptions: in the essay "Of Empire" merchants are described as "*Vena porta*; And if they flourish not, a Kingdome may have good Limmes, but will have empty Veines, and nourish little."[3] But Bacon's concern is with the idea of the ruler as physician maintaining the health of the body politic. In the *History of Henry VII*, the king, "who commonly drew blood as physicians doe", was merciful to the defeated Cornish supporters of Perkin Warbeck.[4] There are "*Mountebanques*" for both the natural and politic bodies: "Men that undertake great Cures; And perhaps have been lucky in two or three Experiments, but want the Grounds of Science...."[5] Neither unlearned doctors nor princes are to be trusted.[6] The ruler must cope with the wounds of heresy and schism and with the inflamed humors of the malcontented.[7] A "moderate Liberty" is the safe way to allow these humors to evaporate; suppression breeds inflammation. Foreign wars are defended as a healthful exercise, to avoid the corruption of manners and loss of courage.[8]

---

[2] J. W. Allen, *English Political Thought: 1603-1644*, (London, 1938), p. 50. In addition to Allen and Bock, I rely on Sabine, *A History of Political Theory*, (New York, 1950), pp. 450-51, and Adolfo Levi, *Il Pensiero di Francesco Bacone* (Turin, 1925), pp. 303-09.

[3] Francis Bacon, *A Harmony of the Essays*, ed. Edward Arber (London, 1871), p. 307.

[4] *The Moral and Historical Works of Lord Bacon*, ed. Joseph Devey, Bohn's Library (London, 1909), p. 435. The passage reappears in the last speech of John Ford's *Perkin Warbeck* (1634):

> [*King Henry.*]   public states,
> As our particular bodies, taste most good
> In health when purged of corrupted blood.

John Ford, *Perkin Warbeck* (V.iii), in: *The Works of John Ford*, ed. Alexander Dyce, 3 vols. (London, 1869), II, 217.

[5] Bacon, "Of Boldness", ed. Arber, p. 519.

[6] Bacon, *The Advancement of Learning*, ed. William A. Wright, 5th ed. (Oxford, 1900), p. 12.

[7] Bacon, "Of Unity in Religion", ed. Arber, p. 423; "Of Seditions and Troubles", pp. 299, 401.

[8] Bacon, "Of the True Greatness of Kingdoms and Estates", ed. Arber, pp. 487, 489. This is only slightly revised from the 1612 text.

These uses of the metaphor of the body politic do not, perhaps, reveal a substantial interest in preserving the unity of the realm. But such was the case. Bacon saw that any attempt to define rigorously the relationship between king and Parliament would lead to trouble. If Bacon is a typical Tudor, it is because he supported the prerogatives of the sovereign and at the same time recognized the futility of seriously antagonizing the Commons.[9] But Bacon's statements are elusive; his principles must be guessed at from his practice.

It is probable that Bacon's use of the organic analogy is illustrative rather than essential.[10] This is a corollary of the attack in his scientific works on the inherited view of nature on which such analogies were based. In one way or another, theories of microcosms contain all of the errors suggested by the four Idols in the *Novum Organum*.

The human understanding, from its peculiar nature, easily supposes a greater degree of order and equality in things than it really finds; and although many things in nature be *sui generis* and most irregular, will yet invent parallels and conjugates and relatives, where no such thing is.[11]

Bacon particularly rejects the followers of Paracelsus, who have "fantastically strained" the concept of man as microcosm to discover absurd correspondences with stars, planets, and minerals.[12] Once such opinions become accepted and used as figures of speech, they are, like the Idols of the Theater, never called into question.[13] Bacon will agree with the Paracelsans only so far as to say that man's body contains the greatest observable complexity and variety of elements.[14]

Having put aside such medieval lumber, Bacon proposes to reinvigorate science, which includes ethics and politics, with a materialism which excludes mind from nature. With Democritus and Descartes, Bacon recognizes only eternal matter and flux or extension.[15] "It is best to consider matter, its conformation, and the changes of that conformation, its own action, and the law of this action or motion; for

[9]   Sabine, *History of Political Thought*, p. 450.
[10]   Conger, *Theories of Macrocosms and Microcosms in the History of Philosophy* (New York, 1922), p. 67.
[11]   Bacon, *Novum Organum* (I, xlv), in *The Physical and Metaphysical Works of Lord Bacon*, ed. Joseph Devey, Bohn's Library (London, 1911), p. 391.
[12]   Bacon, *Advancement of Learning*, p. 134.
[13]   Bacon, *Advancement of Learning*, p. 87. See also F. H. Anderson, *The Philosophy of Francis Bacon* (Chicago, 1948), pp. 141, 167-68.
[14]   Bacon, *The Wisdom of the Ancients*, in: *Moral and Historical Works*, pp. 49-50; *Advancement of Learning*, p. 134.
[15]   Levi, *Il Pensiero di Francesco Bacone*, pp. 223-26; Anderson, *The Philosophy of Francis Bacon*, p. 48.

forms are a mere fiction of the human mind, unless you will call the laws of action by that name."[16] Only on this basis can one build a true model of the world. If form is only the pattern of motion of matter, then any meaningful analogy between the body natural and the body politic is impossible. For Bacon, there were no observable facts to support such an association. The gradual triumph of scientific materialism in the seventeenth century is an indirect but very important factor in the history of the metaphor of the body politic.

"I am the Husband, and all the whole Isle is my lawfull Wife; I am the Head, and it is my Body. . . ."[17] Thus spoke the new king to his Parliament. Two years later he told the Houses that "It is composed of a Head and a Body: The Head is the King, the Body are the members of the Parliament", words which echo the declaration of Henry VIII.[18] The writings of James I are liberally sprinkled with such comparisons of himself to the head of a body. He was also a physician who could cure such infirmities as his subjects' proclivity for smoking tobacco.[19] He defined both his privileges and his obligations in these terms. Yet in his exaltation of his privileges and qualification of his obligations, James extended the absolutism of the Tudors to such a degree and in such a manner as to strike a blow at the unity of the body of the realm. It is important to keep in mind the differences between what the king claimed, what he attempted, and what he accomplished. He attempted, with less success, nothing that had not been done, or could not have been done, by Elizabeth. But in his books and speeches he claimed authority to reverse a century of constitutional development.

The Trew Law of Free Monarchies: or the Reciprock and Mutuall

[16]   Bacon, *Novum Organum* (I, li), in: *Physical and Metaphysical Works*, p. 395.
[17]   James I, "Speech of 1603", in *The Political Works of James I*, ed. Charles H. McIlwain (Cambridge, Mass., 1918), p. 272; for a similar fusion of metaphor, see Bishop Fisher's sermon against Luther, above p. 50. In addition to the literature cited below, I rely on Allen, *English Political Thought: 1603-1660*, pp. 3-25; Sabine, *History of Political Theory*, pp. 395-97; and Helena M. Chew, "King James I", in *The Social and Political Ideas of Some Great Thinkers of the Sixteenth and Seventeenth Centuries*, ed. F. J. C. Hearnshaw (London, 1926), pp. 105-29.
[18]   James I, "Speech of 1605", *Political Works*, p. 287. Compare Shakespeare, *2 Henry IV*, V.ii.134-37:
        [*King Henry V.*]   Now call we our high court of parliament;
        And let us choose such limbs of noble counsel
        That the great body of our state may go
        In equal rank with the best govern'd nation. . . .
[19]   James I, *A Counterblaste to Tobacco* (1604), in: *A Royal Rhetorician*, ed. Robert S. Rait (New York, 1900), p. 32. See also James' remark that the expanding metropolis of London is like the spleen, whose increase wastes the body ("Speech in Star Chamber, 1616", *Political Works*, p. 343).

Duetie Betwixt a Free King, and His Naturall Subjects was published in Edinburgh in 1598 and reprinted in London in 1603; it contains the theory of the divine right of kings in complete detail.[20] The subtitle is revealing. A natural subject has the duty of passive obedience not unlike that proclaimed by the Tudor publicists. A free king's duties are like those of a father of children and a head of a body. There is a long passage detailing how the head provides direction and judgement for the members, orders the functions of the various parts, and cures or cuts off infections.[21] But as a free king, he is not concerned with the elements which unify head and members. The Tudors had inspired the affection and appealed to the common interests of their subjects and had thereby secured their effective cooperation. In theory and in practice the Stuarts did not do very well with either. A ruler bound only by his sense of duty is not really bound at all.[22] James categorically denied the existence of anything resembling a social contract; even if the coronation oath were such an agreement, none but God should judge its violation.[23] In an oft-quoted speech to Parliament in 1609, he declared, "The State of *Monarchy* is the supremest thing upon earth: For Kings are not onely *Gods* Lieutenants upon earth, and sit upon *Gods* throne, but even by *God* himselfe they are called Gods."[24] It is therefore sedition to debate the limits of the royal power. Aristotle might wonder if such a creature were fit for human society.

Medieval kingship had been, in theory, tightly limited by the law. The Tudors worked their will through acts of Parliament, thereby retaining at least a legal façade. But James says that "the King is above the law, as both the author and giver of strength thereto . . ."[25] though he ought politically to conform to it. He concludes that "generall lawes, made publikely in Parliament, may upon knowen respects to the King by his authoritie bee mitigated, and suspended upon causes onely knowen to him".[26] The royal prerogative had been previously regarded as beginning where the law stopped; now prerogative and sovereignty were identified. The Common Law, often called the unifying sinews or soul of the body politic, was subject to the king's whim.

[20]   J. Neville Figgis, *The Divine Right of Kings*, 2nd ed. (Cambridge, 1922), p. 138.
[21]   James I, *Trew Law, Political Works*, pp. 64-65.
[22]   Harold J. Laski, "The Political Ideas of James I", *The Foundations of Sovereignty and Other Essays* (New York, 1921), p. 303.
[23]   James I, *Trew Law, Political Works*, p. 68.
[24]   James I, "Speech of 1609", *Political Works*, p. 307.
[25]   James I, *Trew Law, Political Works*, p. 63.
[26]   James I, *Trew Law, Political Works*, p. 63.

This was Sir John Forescue's *dominium regale*, that which made slaves of Frenchmen; there was a revival of interest in Fortescue in the early seventeenth century.[27]

The Trew Law of Free Monarchies may have inspired some of the talk about the body politic in the works discussed at the end of the preceding chapter. Neither Bacon's materialism nor James' absolutism had much immediately noticeable effect on the core of meaning in the metaphor. Much of the Paracelsan extravagance disappeared rather quickly, but the decline of quantity and seriousness in the analogy, and the related correspondences, was gradual. Perhaps many agreed with Sir Thomas Browne: "but to call our selves a Microcosme, or little world, I thought it onely a pleasant trope of Rhetorick, till my nearer judgement and second thoughts told me there was a recall truth therein. . . ."[28]

A case in point is Robert Burton's *Anatomy of Melancholy*. Bacon's Democritus understood the material nature of the world; Democritus Junior was more interested in man. From his Oxford study, Burton devoted his life to assembling a vast compendium of information about man and the world in which he lived. The first words of the first partition apostrophize "Man the most excellent and noble creature of the world, *the principal and mighty work of God . . . Microcosmos*, a little world . . . created to God's own *Image*, to that immortal and incorporeal substance, with all the faculties and powers belonging unto it. . . ."[29] But as a result of Adam's fall, the universal human condition is melancholy – "*a kind of dotage without a fever, having for his ordinary companions fear and sadness, without any apparent occasion*".[30] Both men and kingdoms are susceptible to the disease. Most of Burton's comments about the maladies of kingdoms are in the Preface, "Democritus Junior to the Reader", which satirizes the follies of men and contains Burton's scheme for a "Utopia" of his own.

> But whereas you shall see many discontents, common grievances, complaints, poverty, barbarism, beggary, plagues, wars, rebellions, seditions, mutinies, contentions, idleness, riot, epicurism, the land lie untilled, waste,

[27] Caroline A. J. Skeel, "The Influence of the Writings of Sir John Fortescue", *Transactions of the Royal Historical Society*, 3rd ser., X (1916), 91-102. Milton cited Fortescue with approval in the *Defensio Prima*; the royalists also found much of use in Fortescue.
[28] Sir Thomas Browne, *Religio Medici* (I, 34), ed. Jean-Jacques Denonain (Cambridge, 1953), p. 53.
[29] Robert Burton, *The Anatomy of Melancholy*, ed. A. R. Shilleto, 3 vols. (London, 1896), I, 149.
[30] Burton, *Anatomy of Melancholy*, I, 150, 193.

full of bogs, fens, deserts, &c., cities decayed, base and poor towns, villages depopulated, the people squalid, ugly, uncivil; that kingdom, that country, must needs be discontent, melancholy, hath a sick body, and had need to be reformed.[31]

Burton does not follow the analogy in detail either in his analysis of contemporary social and economic conditions or in his Utopia. But his ideal kingdom reproduces many of the features of those of the earlier humanists. A proper proportion must be maintained between the various parts of society; there must not be too many lawyers or clergymen. Each class will have a clearly defined function to be performed conscientiously. Foreign trade is to be encouraged; foreign wars discouraged.[32] The unifying element in the kingdom, as in the family, is love: "this is true Love indeed, the cause of all good to mortal men, that reconciles all creatures, and glues them together in perpetual amity and firm league. . . ."[33]

Politics were not absent from the Jacobean and Caroline stage; the obligations and privileges of rulers and subjects are the starting place for many a play. Yet these problems seldom suggest traditional images and metaphors to Webster or Massinger or Beaumont and Fletcher. Murders, wars, and treasons are imagined in more personal terms, without reference to an accepted social pattern which is being disrupted. Love and honor become more important than order and degree; the poetry of the plays reflects this change. Nevertheless, examples of the idea of the body politic may be found. In Fletcher and Massinger's *The Double Marriage* (*ca.* 1620) Sesse addresses Ascanio, the new King of Naples:

> [*Sesse.*]   Learn that you are to govern men, not beasts:
> And that is a most improvident head,
> That strives to hurt the limbs that do support it.[34]

The Duke Florence, in *The Fair Maid of the Inn* (1625) by Ford and Massinger, has to put a stop to the fighting between two families:

---

[31]   Burton, *Anatomy of Melancholy*, I, 87.
[32]   Burton's schemes are summarized in detail in William R. Mueller, *The Anatomy of Robert Burton's England*, University of California Publications in English Studies No. 2 (Berkeley & Los Angeles, 1952), pp. 33-63. Burton seems to have been well acquainted with contemporary economic literature. See also J. Max Patrick, "Robert Burton's Utopianism", *Philological Quarterly*, XXVII (1948), 345-58.
[33]   Burton, *Anatomy of Melancholy*, III, 35.
[34]   *The Double Marriage* (V.i.), *The Works of Francis Beaumont and John Fletcher*, ed. Arnold Glover and A. R. Waller, 10 vols. (Cambridge, 1905-12), VI, 407. I accept the dates and authorship given by G. C. Macaulay in his chapter on "Beaumont and Fletcher" in the *Cambridge History of English Literature*.

[*Duke.*]   *Baptista* ... the petty brawls and quarrels
Late urg'd betwixt th' Alberti and your family;
Must, yes, and shall, like tender unknit joynts,
Fasten again together of themselves:
Or like an angry Chyrurgion, we will use
The roughness of our justice, to cut off
The stubborn rancour of the limbes offending.[35]

In 1627 Thomas Middleton wrote a pageant called *The Triumphs of Health and Prosperity* to celebrate the inauguration of Cuthbert Hacket as Lord Mayor of London. There is a speech praising the city and describing its place in the structure of the kingdom:

With just propriety does this city stand,
As fix'd by fate, i' the middle of the land;
It has, as in the body, the heart's place,
Fit for her works of piety and grace. . . .[36]

The king is the head, receiving "All duties that just service comprehends". The eyes are counselors, the lips are clergy and judges, and the arms are "the defensive part of men". As the heart is the first organ to receive life and the last to die, London is first in the affections of the king and to him shows more loyalty than any other city.[37]

Two essentially nonpolitical examples may be cited from seventeenth-century poets. In the "Funerall Elegie" in *An Anatomie of the World* (1611), John Donne writes of the effects of the death of Elizabeth Drury:

The world containes
Princes for armes, and Cousailors for braines,
Lawyers for tongues, Divines for hearts and more,
The Rich for stomachs, and for backes the Pore;
The Officers for hands, Merchants for feet
By which remote and distant Countries meet.
But those fine spirits which doe tune and set
This Organ, are those peeces which beget

[35] *The Fair Maid of the Inn* (III.i), in: *Works of Beaumont and Fletcher*, IX, 178. See also the passage in which two brothers are told that they are "like mutual legs/ Supplanting one another" and are urged to co-operate like eyes or ears ([Fletcher and Massinger] *The Queen of Corinth* [1617], in: *Works of Beaumont and Fletcher*, VI, 63). This passage echoes Xenophon's *Memorabilia* (above, pp. 22-23).
[36] Thomas Middleton, *The Triumphs of Health and Prosperity*, in: *The Works of Thomas Middleton*, ed. A. H. Bullen, 8 vols. (London, 1885-86), VII, 408.
[37] Middleton, *Triumphs of Health and Prosperity*, *Works*, VII, 409. See also the extensive passages in *The Wisdom of Solomon Paraphrased* (1597), *Works*, VIII, 172-73, 284.

> Wonder and love; And these were shee; and shee
> Being spent, the world must needes decrepit bee.[38]

This is the pathetic fallacy, of course, but it is an ingenious adaptation of traditional discussions of the structure of the body politic. A similar conceit appears in Thomas Carew's "Upon the Kings Sicknesse":

> But now the Tyrant hath found out a way
> By which the sober, strong, and young, decay:
> Entring his royall limbes that is our head,
> Through us his mystique limbs the paine is spread,
> That man that doth not feele his part, hath none
> In any part of his dominion. . . .[39]

The sufferings of a King are felt by all his subjects.

Perhaps the decline of the metaphor of the body politic may be seen most clearly in the works of those who defended the royalist position during the reign of Charles I. In turn they urged the nation to unity and obedience and then lamented the calamity of civil war and regicide. The writers who supported the king had only to restate an established position; what they did have to offer that was new were very hesitant gestures in the direction of royal absolutism.[40] Old idea encouraged old language; the metaphor of the body politic was used by many, but briefly and without the vividness or originality found earlier.

A good example is found in a sermon by William Laud, then Bishop of St. David's, preached at the opening of Parliament in February, 1626. There is a double unity in the state – the body with the head and the members with each other. This two-fold relationship, which the Puritans established by a contract, is here presented as being in the nature of the body politic.[41] Quoting I Corinthians XII, Laud says that St. Paul can imagine "how corruption can unnaturalize nature itself" in a dangerous quarrel between the eye and the hand; the head, nevertheless, can pacify them. "And yet the Apostle cannot suppose so much unnaturalness that any member should quarrel the 'head'; not the 'tongue', as unruly as it is. . . ."[42] And if the Parliament would preserve

[38]   John Donne, *The Anniversaries*, ed. Frank Manley (Baltimore, 1963), pp. 82-83.
[39]   Thomas Carew, *The Poems of Thomas Carew*, ed. Rhodes Dunlap (Oxford, 1949), p. 35. These lines refer to the fatal illness of King James in 1625 (p. 229).
[40]   See in general Allen, *English Political Thought: 1603-1644*, pp. 482-519, and Perez Zagorin, *A History of Political Thought in the English Revolution* (London, pp. 189-202.
[41]   Williams Laud, "A Sermon Preached . . . at Westminster", *The Works of Archbishop Laud*, ed. William Scott, 9 vols., Library of Anglo-Catholic Theology (Oxford, 1847-57), I, 69. Cf. Milton, *Tenure of Kings and Magistrates* (see below, p. 125).
[42]   Laud, "A Sermon Preached . . . at Westminster", *Works*, I, 70.

the unity of the State, the peace of the Church must not be disturbed with divisive arguments about salvation. This unity of Church and State is proclaimed in a sermon before King James in 1621:

[A man] must live in the body of the Commonwealth. and in the body of the Church; and if their joints be out, and in trouble, how can he hope to live in "peace"? This is just as if the exterior parts of the body should think they might live healthful, though the stomach be full of sick and swollen humours.[43]

To a later Parliament (1628) Laud says that the Church, like the soul, unifies the members of the bodies politic and natural.[44]

Laud's sermon set the pattern for two decades of exhortation by clergy and laymen. An instance is a sermon preached at Paul's Cross in 1629 by one Richard Farmer.[45] Taking I Corinthians XII as his text, Farmer fills his sermon with organic imagery and pleads for national unity. Events, however, were contrary; increasing dissatisfaction with foreign policy, finances, and church government produced warfare in which first ink flowed, and then blood. The taking up of swords did not stop the scratching of pens; the king's pamphleteers continued to plead for obedience.

Sir John Spelman carefully defines two natures of man; kingdoms are not associations of individuals, but communions of men "*quatenus membres politique*" united in obedience.[46] Each member of the body, from head to foot, has an assigned "office politique" which he ought to execute. Henry Ferne continues the argument by denying that Parliament is defending the nation by protecting itself: "As the naturall body defends it self against an outward force, but strives not by a schisme or contentation within it self; so may the body politick against an outward power, but not as now by one part of it set against the Head and another part of the same party; for that tends to the dissolution of the whole."[47] It is clear that the current distempers are such a dissolution.[48] Francis Quarles, the writer of emblem books, composed several tracts in defence of the King. To Parliament's assertion of superiority because

<hr>

[43] Laud, "A Sermon Preached Before His Majesty", *Works*, I, 29.
[44] Laud, "A Sermon Preached at Westminster", *Works*, I, 164. See pp. 169-70, 176-77.
[45] Richard Farmer, *A Sermon Preached at Pauls Crosse* (London, 1629).
[46] John Spelman, *Certain Considerations Upon the Dueties both of Prince and People* (Oxford, 1642), sig. A3.
[47] Henry Ferne, *The Resolving of Conscience upon this Question* (Cambridge, 1642), sig. A4v.
[48] Ferne, *The Resolving of Conscience*, sig. Dlv.

of its representative character, Quarles replies, "If our blessed Saviour be not *Representative*, Tell me whereof art thou a Member? Woe be to that Body *politick*, which endeavours not to be conformed according to the Head Mysticall."[49] Woe indeed, for Parliament was out to prove a claim that it was "that to the Commonwealth which the soul is to the body".[50]

The shock of the Civil War was a serious affliction to the body of the realm. To John Cleveland a follower of Parliament was "the spleen of the body politic that swells itself to the consumption of the whole".[51] In Quarles' *The New Distemper* (1645) dismay becomes anguish. He recognizes that there is need for reform, that the discipline and government of the Church are diseased with evil manners and foul humours bred of neglect.[52] Triennial Parliaments may be an effective and gradual cure. But to those conducting a reformation in root and branch he says, "Take heed while ye goe about to cure a *Fever*, you run not the Body Politick into a *Dropsie*, with too much *Phlebotomie*."[53] England has come to such a distempered condition that there is a temptation to try to cure it with a desperate remedy. "Look, O look back into the blessed dayes of Queene *Elizabeth*: Observe what blessings we then had. . . ."[54] The distemper was such that it could only be cured by the army, "the only and alone salve to heal and cure the wounds of this distracted and dying Nation. . . ."[55] The New Model's remedy, however, was described by an anonymous poet:

> . . . these Acephalists, who here in stead
> Of Prince, set up a State without an Head.
> Must *Feet* pronounce a sentence on their *Head*,
> And reare *imposthum'd members* in his stead?[56]

---

[49]   Francis Quarles, *The Loyall Convert* (1643), *The Complete Works in Prose and Verse*, ed. Alexander B. Grosart, 3 vols., Chertsey Worthies' Library (Edinburgh, 1880), I, 142.

[50]   'King' John Pym to the Short Parliament, quoted in Godfrey Davies, *The Early Stuarts: 1603-1660*, 2nd ed. (Oxford, 1959), p. 93.

[51]   John Cleveland, "The Character of a County Committeeman" (1649), in: *Character Writings of the Seventeenth Century*, ed. Henry Morley (London, 1891), p. 300.

[52]   Quarles, *The New Distemper, Complete Works*, I, 148.

[53]   Quarles, *The New Distemper, Complete Works*, I, 153. The fear of excessive 'phlebotomie' echoes James Howell, *England's Teares, for the Present Wars* (London, 1644), sig. B2.

[54]   Quarles, *The New Distemper, Complete Works*, I, 156.

[55]   John Lilburne, *The Legall Fundamentall Liberties of the People of England* (1649), in: *The Leveller Tracts: 1647-1653*, ed. William A. Haller and Godfrey Davies (New York, 1944), p. 442.

[56]   "Albions Niobe", in *The Princely Pelican* (n.p., 1649), sig. F2r-v.

Richard Lovelace wrote bitterly:

> Now *Whitehalls* in the grave,
> And our *Head* is our slave
>   Now the *Thighs* of the Crown,
>   And the *Arms* are lopp'd down,
>   And the *Body* is all but a *Belly*. . . .[57]

The fable of the belly and the rebellious members continued to appear. Bacon regarded the tales of Aesop as a kind of 'parabolical wisdom' used to convey subtle or abstract ideas by men living in a time which lacked more sophisticated means of expression.[58] As in the preceding century, varying applications were given the fable, but these applications were less imaginative and less conservative.

Between 1600 and 1660 the fable of the belly appeared in twenty collections of Aesopic fables in English, Latin, or both. Caxton's translation was reprinted in 1628, 1634, 1647, and 1658. The rendering by William Barret (1639), the first illustrated collection in English verse, provides a specifically political moral:

> Look what estate we in our body see,
> The same concordance must in Kingdomes be;
> Friends must their friends support and all unite,
> T'uphold the chief. Lest while his good they slight,
>   If in the State a dissolution grow,
>   They pluck on them a generall overthrow.[59]

There is a woodcut of the starved body, like that in Caxton but drawn in more detail and emphasizing the walled city in the background. Even more topical is the version by John Ogilby (1651, 1668). The Stomach rules only after "*Reason*, once King in Man", is deposed; the Members, "who now turn Levellers", rebel against the tyrannical appetite and, as the Body dies, reflect that their first mistake was dethroning Reason.[60] The full-page engraving shows a lively, but decapitated body, with a

[57] Richard Lovelace, "A Mock-Song", *The Poems of Richard Lovelace*, ed. C. H. Wilkinson (Oxford, 1930), pp. 154-55. Lovelace alludes to the tearing down of the royal coat of arms ordered in February, 1649 (p. 311); the wound in the thigh implies castration.
[58] Bacon, *Advancement of Learning*, pp. 102-3. Several of the interpretations of classical myths given by Bacon in *The Wisdom of the Ancients* are explicitly political.
[59] *The Fables of Aesop* (London, 1639), sig. K3ᵛ. Compare the similar but more elegant fable and engraving in *Les Fables d'Esope Phrygien*, trans. Jean Baudoin (Paris, 1631), pp. 246-249. In an anonymously expanded version (1650), Barret's text was reprinted frequently in the second half of the century.
[60] *The Fables of Aesop, Paraphrased in Verse*, ed. Earl Miner, Augustan Reprint Society (Los Angeles, 1965), pp. 114-116.

face on the oversize belly. Ogilby has mechanically united the traditions which locate authority in either the belly or the head to produce an allegory forecasting chaos after the death of Charles I. Other verse translations, of less interest, were published by R.A. (1634) and Leonard Willan (1650).

The fable was turned to several purposes. Burton mentions Menenius' use of the "elegant Apologue" as a remedy against the discontent of the "tumultuous rout of *Rome*" who would have all men idle and of equal wealth.[61] Bacon compared the misguided members of the body to those who disparage the seemingly useless study of philosophy; but, like the stomach, learning serves and supplies all the other professions.[62]

The most politically significant use of the fable is John Milton's in *Of Reformation Touching Church-Discipline in England* (1641), the first of his tracts against the bishops. Milton distills his opinion of the prelates into Menenius' little tale:

Upon a time the Body [England] summon'd all the Members to meet in the Guild [Parliament] for the common good ... the head [Charles I] by right takes the first seat, and next to it a huge and monstrous Wen [the episcopacy] little lesse then the Head it selfe, growing to it by a narrower excrescency.[63]

The Wen, "though unweildy", tells the assembly that it is "second to the head, so by due of merit" and "an ornament, and strength' to it. "Therefore hee thought it for the honour of the Body, that such dignities and rich indowments should be decreed him, as did adorne, and set out the noblest Members." The assembly summons "a wise and learned Philosopher [a proposed parliamentary commission, or Commons? or Milton?] ... that knew all the Charters, Lawes, and Tenures of the Body". He is charged to examine the Wen's claims to honors and subsidies, but soon discovers the true nature of "such a swolne Tumor". "Wilt thou ... that art but a bottle of vitious and harden'd excrements, contend with the lawful and free-borne members, whose certaine number is set by ancient and unrepealable Statute? Head thou art none, though thou receive this huge substance from it, what office bearst thou? What good canst thou shew by thee done to the Common-weale?" The Wen tries to defend itself, but the Philosopher declares "that thou containst no good thing in thee, but a heape of hard, and loathsome un-

[61] Burton, *Anatomy of Melancholy*, II, 196. Menenius is also mentioned in I, 406.
[62] Bacon, *Advancement of Learning*, p. 78.
[63] John Milton, *Of Reformation*, in: *The Works of John Milton*, gen. ed. Frank A. Patterson, 21 vols. (New York, 1931-38), III, pt. i, 47-48.

cleannes, and art to the head a foul disfigurment and burden, when I have cut thee off, and open'd thee . . . all men shall see." [64]

There are several observations to be made on this attack on the prelates. Milton has rearranged considerably the elements from Aesop and Menenius. Traditionally the members rebel against the vital belly, which is able in debate or by withholding nourishment to defend itself. But the fable is now an exemplum justifying a piece of surgery which the king himself ought to perform. This is the antithesis of a passage in Bishop Joseph Hall's *Episcopacy by Divine Right*, published the year before: "We cut off a limb to prevent the deadly malignity of a gangrene: is this any warrant to dismember the sound?" [65] And Thomas Fuller described a good bishop as one who approaches heretics as a physician treats lepers, varying the treatment to the infectiousness of the disease. [66] Milton argues at length that the bishops are not functional members of the body politic, but mere cancerous growths; this is a startling reapplication of the idea that it is the king's duty to remove infected parts. Traditional expressions here advocate revolutionary practice.

Indeed, supporting Tillyard's observation that Milton's first pamphlets are his most scholarly and most directly connected to the political thought of the Renaissance, we find a considerable amount of talk about the body politic in Milton's tracts of 1641. [67] He is calling for changes to be made within the established order. But by the end of the decade much water and blood had flowed under the bridge. Milton was given the responsibility of defending the execution of the king; this he did through recourse to the idea of a covenant, a social contract.

[64] Milton, *Of Reformation, Works*, III, pt. i, 49.
[65] Joseph Hall, *Episcopacy by Divine Right*, in *The Works of the Right Reverend Joseph Hall*, ed. Philip Wynter, 10 vols. (Oxford, 1863), IX, 156. In his earlier devotional and controversial writings Hall used organic analogies with some frequency; they are rare in his works against the Smectymnuans.
[66] Thomas Fuller, "The Good Bishop", *The Holy State and the Profane State* (1642), ed. Maximilian G. Walten, 2 vols., Columbia University Studies in English and Comparative Literature No. 136 (New York, 1938), II, 279. Fuller reproduces an idea which had been used before; see Nashe (above, p. 82).
[67] E. M. W. Tillyard, *Milton* (London, 1930), pp. 119, 126. Milton's political ideas are discussed in the valuable introductions in *Complete Prose Works of John Milton*, gen. ed. Don M. Wolfe, 8 vols. (New Haven, 1953–). See also Zera S. Fink, *The Classical Republicans*, Northwestern University Studies in the Humanities No. 9 (Evanston, 1945); William Haller, *Liberty and Reformation in the Puritan Revolution* (New York, 1955); Raven I. McDavid, "Milton as a Political Thinker", unpublished dissertation (Duke University, 1935); and Don M. Wolfe, *Milton in the Puritan Revolution* (New York, 1941).

Milton's political writings form, as it were, a sort of microcosm in themselves.

Milton speaks both of the body of the kingdom and of "that immortall stature of Christs body which is his Church in all her glorious lineaments and proportions".[68] In the earliest days of Christianity, "then did the Spirit of unity and meeknesse inspire, and animate every joynt, and sinew of the mysticall body. . . ."[69] This purity of doctrine and worship has been corrupted by the bishops who dressed the body of the church with palls and mitres and "guegaw's fetcht from *Arons* old wardrope" until the soul has given itself up to the delights of the flesh.[70] The episcopal establishment is likened to "hydropick humors" which are not seen at first in a fair body, but which, if unchecked, will produce a universal rottenness and gangrene.[71]

Similarly, Milton refers to Aristotle in defining the state:

A Commonwelth ought to be but as one huge Christian personage, one mighty growth, and stature of an honest man, as big, and compact in vertue as in body; for looke what the grounds, and causes are of single happines to one man, the same yee shall find them to a whole state. . . .[72]

Since spiritual and secular realms are inseparable, it becomes the duty of the prince, as physician, to take action against "the noysom, and diseased tumor of Prelacie . . .".[73]

[This is] a saving med'cin ordain'd of God . . . if he [the magistrate] find in his [the body politic's] complexion, skin, or outward temperature the signes and marks, or in his doings the effects of injustice, rapine, lust, cruelty, or the like, sometimes he shuts up as in frenetick, or infectious diseases. . . . Sometimes he shaves by penalty, or mulct, or els to cool and take down those luxuriant humors which wealth and excesse have caus'd to abound. Otherwhiles he seres, he cauterizes, he scarifies, lets blood and finally for utmost remedy cuts off.[74]

But by 1649 the case was much altered. The army had done what the king had not; it became Milton's task to defend Cromwell and the Rump Parliament against the condemnation of the world. The first

---

[68]   Milton, *The Reason of Church-Government Urg'd Against Prelaty, Works*, III, pt. i, 191. In *De Doctrina Christiana* Milton quotes St. Paul extensively to define the mystical body of Christ (*Works*, XVI, 57-65).

[69]   Milton, *Of Reformation, Works*, III, pt. i, 18.

[70]   Milton, *Of Reformation, Works*, III, pt. i, 2.

[71]   Milton, *Animadversions Upon the Remonstrants Defence Against Smectymnus, Works*, III, pt. i, 117.

[72]   Milton, *Of Reformation, Works*, III, pt. i, 38.

[73]   Milton, *Of Reformation, Works*, III, pt. i, 62.

[74]   Milton, *Reason of Church-Government, Works*, III, pt. i, 254-55.

step was the hurried and unsuccessful *Eikonoklastes*, an attempt to answer *Eikon Basilike: The Pourtraiture of His Sacred Majestie in His Solitudes and Sufferings*, which had appeared shortly after the death of the king and was believed to have been written by him. *Eikon Basilike* draws heavily on the traditional imagery associated with kingship, especially that of the king as sun or shepherd; Milton dismisses this as the habit of bad poets. In *Eikon Basilike* there is no extensive use of the metaphor of the body politic, but in the discussion of the death of Sir John Hotham (1645) there is a passing reference to the king as "the head of the Commonweal".[75] Milton summarizes the passage to show how the comparison is handled: "*two heads cut off in one family for affronting the head of the Common-wealth; the eldest son being infected with the sins of his Father, against the Father of his Countrie.*"[76] Then he completely denies the validity of such analogical thinking: "These petty glosses and conceits . . . are so weak and shallow, and so like the quibbl's of a Court Sermon, that we may safely reck'n them either fetcht from such a pattern, or that the hand of some household priest foisted them in. . . ."[77] Similarly, in the *Defensio Prima* Milton dismisses as "flippant" Salmasius' (and James') contention that the king, like the head, is to command Parliament, the members.[78] Only a few years before Milton himself had indulged in "these petty glosses and conceits"; now they are "quibbl's".

This is the vehement conclusion of a process of questioning the applicability of organic analogies to political problems. Earlier in the century Bishop Hall met a Brownist contention that if the tongue (clergy) spoke ill, the whole man (Church) sinned:

. . . you shall set the natural body on too hard a rack of you strain it in all things to the likeness of the spiritual or civil. The members of that, being quickened by the same soul, have charge of each other; and therefore either stand or fall together. It is not so in these.[79]

Hall goes no further; yet he seems to have been forced to deny the validity of I Corinthians XII. On the continent Hugo Grotius saw both similarities and differences between natural and politic bodies, among them the contractual origin of the state and the right of a part to protect

---

[75] *Eikon Basilike*, ed. Edward J. L. Scott (London, 1880), p. 40.
[76] Milton, *Eikonoklastes, Works*, V, 146-47. See Ernest Sirluck, "Milton's Political Thought: The First Cycle", *Modern Philology*, LXI (1964), 209-24.
[77] Milton, *Eikonoklastes, Works*, V, 147.
[78] Milton, *Pro Populo Anglicano Defensio*, trans. Samuell L. Wolff, *Works*, VII, 419; hereafter *Defensio Prima*.
[79] Hall, *Epistles in Six Decades*, III (1611), *Works*, VI, 293.

itself against the body.[80] In 1642 Henry Parker observed that

... the head naturally doth not more depend upon the body, than that does upon the head, both head and members must live and die together; but it is otherwise with the Head Politicall, for that receives more subsistence from the body than it gives, and being subservient to that, it has no being when that is dissolved, and that may be preserved after its dissolution.[81]

The body politic may safely be decapitated because the analogy is invalid.

So Milton turns to the idea of a covenant, the violation of which justifies the deposition of the king. In *Eikonoklastes* he defines a commonwealth not with the physiological imagery of the body politic, but with abstractions:

... a societie sufficient of it self, in all things conducible to well being and commodious life. Any of which requisit things if it cannot have without the gift and favour of a single person on without leave of his private person, or his conscience, it cannot be thought sufficient of it self, and by consequence, no Common-wealth. . . .[82]

The concept of a covenant is, indeed, found in earlier pamphlets. In *The Doctrine and Discipline of Divorce* (1643), Milton compares marriage and a citizen's oath of allegiance as examples of similar covenants.[83] The differences between them, at this stage in the development of Milton's thought, is that God explicitly permits the marital contract to be broken, while no such sanction exists for the victims of tyranny.

Milton sees the king's power as being limited in two ways: by a covenant represented by the coronation oath, and by the law. Milton, like the French monarchomachs, regards the social contract as a two-step process. The sin of Adam brought misery and violence to all men.

---

[80]   Cited in Gierke, *Natural Law and the Theory of Society*, trans. Ernest Barker, 2 vols. (Cambridge, 1934), II, 253.

[81]   Henry Parker, *Observations upon some of his Majesties late Answers and Expresses*, in: *Tracts on Liberty in the Puritan Revolution: 1638-1647*, ed. William Haller, 3 vols. (New York, 1934), II, 185. Cf. John Wildman's answer to Sir John Maynard: "I hope the gentleman will please to confess a vast difference between a body natural and a body politic" (*London's Liberties* [1650], in *Puritanism and Liberty*, ed. A.S.P. Woodhouse [Chicago, 1951], p. 375).

[82]   Milton, *Eikonoklastes, Works*, V, 175-76.

[83]   Milton, *The Doctrine and Discipline of Divorce, Works*, III, pt. ii, 374-75. Also, in *De Doctrina Christina*, Milton describes the visible church, as opposed to the mystical, as being held together by its discipline: "a mutual agreement among the members of the church, to fashion their lives according to Christian doctrine . . ." (*Works*, XVI, 321).

Then, "Forseeing that such courses must needs tend to the destruction of them all, they agreed by common league to bind each other from mutual injury, and joyntly to defend themselves against any that gave disturbance or opposition to such agreement."[84] This is the origin of towns, cities, and commonwealths. Afterwards the people voluntarily consented to give authority to kings and magistrates as a means of effecting this agreement.[85] The people's oaths of allegiance signify their acceptance of the contract. When the king violates the terms of the agreement and thereby becomes a tyrant, the agreement is no longer binding on his subjects.[86] The judge of this violation, always a difficult point in such arguments, is to be Parliament in its capacity as the highest court in the realm.[87]

As part of the agreement establishing kings and magistrates, the peoples established the law above the rulers and exacted solemn oaths from the rulers that they would obey and enforce the laws.[88] Milton explicitly denies the Stuart claim, urged by Salmasius, that kings are above the law; the law which punishes all men also punishes kings.[89] Milton is vague about the nature of the law, but he seems to distinguish two types. The law of England, the Common Law, is the creation of the people through the traditional machinery, especially the king in Parliament. Natural law, apparently identified with the law of God, justifies a people's defending themselves against a tyrannical prince.[90] It is the law which has made Parliament equal, even superior, to kings.[91] In the *Defensio Prima*, Milton adduces lengthy historical arguments to prove that Parliament is not the creation of the monarch, but an expression of the popular will; kings are the servants of their subjects, not their masters.[92] The underlying principle is that "The right of the people is as much from God as is the right of the king – whatever that is."[93]

In his metamorphosis from employing the analogy of the body politic

---

[84] Milton, *The Tenure of Kings and Magistrates* (1649), *Works*, V, 8.
[85] Milton, *Tenure of Kings and Magistrates, Works*, V, 8, 30. See also *Defensio Prima, Works*, VII, 209.
[86] Milton, *Tenure of King and Magistrates, Works*, V, 55; also *Defensio Prima, Works*, VII, 209 and 265, citing examples from Frankish history.
[87] Milton, *Eikonoklastes, Works*, V, 299.
[88] Milton, *Tenure of Kings and Magistrates, Works*, V, 9.
[89] Milton, *Defensio Prima, Works*, VII, 71, 79.
[90] Milton, *Tenure of Kings and Magistrates, Works*, V, 55.
[91] Milton, *Defensio Prima, Works*, VII, 253.
[92] Milton, *Defensio, Prima, Works*, VII, 419, 157-59.
[93] Milton, *Defensio Prima, Works*, VII, 113.

to asserting the contractual nature of the state, Milton passed through several phases of opinion. From supporting reform within the established order to defending revolution, he denied all of the usual ideas associated with the organic metaphor – a divinely – ordered hierarchy, authoritarian government, religious conformity, and ecclesiastical unity. It is indeed paradoxical that much of what he rejected in his prose he accepted magnificently in his poetry.[94] There is no parallel between Satan's rebellion and Parliament's; Charles I is no crucified Christ.[95]

Milton's works gave official sanction to ideas which had been expressed before both in England and on the Continent.[96] The contractual nature of society and the right of resistance by force of arms were proclaimed in defence of Parliament and the New Model Army. Covenant and contract were already embedded in the instruments of government of the colonies in New England; some settlers, such as Roger Williams, and their books crossed the ocean to find new audiences in England.[97] "The sovereign original and foundation of civil power lies in the people" who may establish whatever form of government they think proper.[98] Particularly striking is Williams' statement that the church, long *corpus mysticum*, is "like unto a corporation, society or company of East India or Turkey merchants . . .".[99]

Resistance and contract are combined in a pasage in the *Table-Talk* of the learned John Selden:

> To know what obedience is due to the prince you must look into the contract betwixt him and his people; as, if you would know what rent is due from the tenant to the landlord, you must look into the lease. When the contract is broken, and there is no third person to judge, the decision is by arms. This is the case between the prince and the subject.[100]

The royalists had argued that there was no judge, except God, of a king's violation of a contract, and therefore passive obedience and

---

[94]   See Malcolm M. Ross, *Milton's Royalism* (Ithaca, N.Y., 1943).
[95]   Milton, *Eikonoklastes, Works*, V, 137.
[96]   Wolfe, *Milton in the Puritan Revolution*, pp. 184-207. See also Gough, *The Social Contract*, pp. 84-104; Allen, *English Political Thought*, pp. 255-481; and Zagorin, *Political Thought in the English Revolution*, pp. 8-105.
[97]   The best acount of covenant theology and its application in the colonies is Perry Miller, *Errand into the Wilderness* (Cambridge, Mass., 1956), pp. 1-15. This essay summarizes the main points of Miller's earlier books.
[98]   Roger Williams, *The Bloody Tenent of Persecution* (1644), in: *Puritanism and Liberty*, ed. Woodhouse, p. 283.
[99]   Williams, *The Bloody Tenent*, in *Puritanism and Liberty*, p. 267.
[100]   John Selden, "War", *John Selden and His Table-Talk*, ed. Robert Waters (New York, 1899), pp. 206-7.

prayer were the only recourses for a subject. Selden's realistic observation circumvents a great amount of verbiage about law and right and
justice; Charles I may have been the victim of unnatural rebels, but at
Naseby the big battalions were not his.

Among the most radical and, through their spokesmen in the army,
temporarily influential were the Levellers, especially John Lilburne.
They carried the idea of a social contract so far as to prepare several
Agreements of the People which were supposed to be taken around the
countryside for signatures as visible evidence of Englishmen's consent
to their form of government.[101] The scheme was squashed by Cromwell. The basic principle of the Levellers was stated by Lilburne: "All
power is originally and essentially in the whole body of the people of
this Nation, and . . . their free choice or consent by their Representatives is the only originall or foundation of all just government. . . ."[102]
Kings are established by the people for their own benefit and may be
deposed; the law, furthermore, is superior to the king, yet inferior to
the people, who are its parent.[103] Only a small minority held such extreme views, but for a while they were able to wield political power;
the indirect influence of their ideas was very great.

The political writings of Thomas Hobbes also reveal the decay of
meaning in the organic analogy, but the evidence is more complicated.
One might expect to find that the similarities between *The Tenure of
Kings and Magistrates and Leviathan* (1651) extend no further than
proximity of dates of publication and the fact that both books were
burned by the University of Oxford in 1683.[104] But Milton, the defender of regicides, and Hobbes, the supporter of royalism, have little
use for the metaphor of the body politic and replace it with a social
contract; it is in the details of the contract that their very great differences appear. And while Milton's rejection of the metaphor was spread
over a decade, the sage of Malmesbury's practice can be found within
the pages of one folio volume. This juxtaposition has puzzled some
and leads Professor Conger to say that in spite of Hobbes' statement

---

[101]   The texts are reprinted in *Leveller Manifestoes of the Puritan Revolution*, ed.
Don. M. Wolfe (New York, 1944), pp. 226-34, 294-303, 400-10.
[102]   John Lilburne, *The Case of the Armie* (1647), in *The Leveller Tracts*, ed. Haller
and Davies, p. 78. See also Richard Overton, *An Appeale* (1647), in *Leveller Manifestoes*, ed. Wolfe, p. 162.
[103]   Thus John Redingstone, *The Peoples Right Briefly Asserted* (1649), quoted in
Wolfe, *Milton in the Puritan Revolution*, p. 200.
[104]   Their diversities are stressed by Don M. Wolfe, "Milton and Hobbes: A Contrast in Social Temper", *Studies in Philology*, XLI (1944), 410-26.

that the body politic is a fiction, "he must attach a certain seriousness to it . . .".[105]

The traditional analogy appears in two ways in *Leviathan*. The lower half of the engraved title page shows a simple landscape containing a town and the surrounding countryside. Coming over the horizon is the giant figure of Leviathan shown from the waist up. His crowned head resembles either Charles I (in the first edition) or Cromwell (in subsequent reprints).[106] The figure holds a sword in one hand and a crosier in the other; his arms and trunk are composed of a great many individual persons, about as tall as the thickness of Leviathan's wrist. This engraving illustrates the idea that the sovereign is the head of a body composed of his subjects and that all spiritual and temporal power is gathered in his hands.

In the manner of Starkey's *Dialogue between Pole and Lupset* Hobbes describes the structure of the state in terms of the parts of the body and the variety of diseases which infect the body. These lists are rather heterogeneous and the comparisons are not insisted upon. Thus sovereignty is the soul of the commonwealth, systems (corporations) are the muscles, public ministers are the organs or nerves, judges are the voice which directs the hands, the eyes are agents abroad, the blood is the gold and silver which flow through the veins or treasury officials.[107] These are operations of government, providing legal and economic protection. The diseases of the state are epilepsy, or the influence of a "Ghostly" religious authority; ague, or the opinion that a subject's rights of property allow him to refuse to pay taxes; pleurisy, or monopolies; and worms, or a multitude of corporations which leads to excessive legal wrangling.[108] All of these diseases impede efficient administration, although Hobbes, unlike Starkey, does not specify the details which make his comparisons appropriate. Hobbes also says that a mixed government with its diffusion of authority would be a monstrosity not unlike Siamese twins.[109]

In contrast to this must be set Hobbes' comments on metaphor and his theory of the origin of the state. If a political philosopher would be scientific, "the use of Metaphors, Tropes, and other Rhetorical figures

[105]   Conger, *Theories of Macrocosms and Microcosms*, p. 69.
[106]   A. R. Waller, Introduction to *Leviathan* (Cambridge, 1904), p. v.
[107]   Hobbes, *Leviathan* (Chs. 21-24), pp. 156, 158, 170-71, 173, 174, 180. A similar scheme is very briefly presented in the "Introduction", p. xviii.
[108]   Hobbes, *Leviathan* (Ch. 29), pp. 238-41.
[109]   Hobbes, *Leviathan*, pp. 239-40.

in stead of words proper" must be eschewed.[110] Therefore Leviathan, the commonwealth, "is but an Artificiall Man" created by the art of man in imitation of nature of God's act of creation.[111] The body politic is "a fictitious body", with fictitious faculties and will.[112] The contract by which men establish the state is like God's willing the creation of man. Like Milton's view that the social contract originated in a period of anarchic violence, Hobbes' contract is response to the primitive condition of war between men when life was "solitary, poore, nasty, brutish, and short".[113] The causes of this situation are different, but the situation is the same. A fear of death leads men to transfer their liberty to someone to rule and protect them.[114] Unlike Milton, Hobbes defines this contract as a one-step process between individual and sovereign, not between a previously united people and ruler.

The details of this covenant are based on quite different premises and are developed to antithetical conclusions. The sovereign is not involved in any submission in accepting the contract; he therefore has no definable obligations to his subjects. Natural law demands obedience; the contract is binding on the subject no matter what the sovereign does. Positive law (Hobbes prefers civil law to common law) is the expression of the will of the sovereign and is in no way binding on him. The Church is subordinate to the state; there is, in this world, no universal church, but a series of particular, national churches under the headship of their respective kings.[115]

Hobbes sees monarchy not as the most natural form of government but as the most perfect artificial state. His insistence upon the artificiality of the state is consistent with his materialistic interpretation of nature. In the second stage of development of the Renaissance view of nature, the world is regarded as being a machine; the progress of this idea, begun by Copernicus, is continued by Galileo, who influenced Hobbes greatly.[116] In the "Introduction" to Leviathan Hobbes draws a

---

[110]   Hobbes, Leviathan (Ch. 5), p. 25.
[111]   Hobbes, Leviathan, p. xviii.
[112]   Thomas Hobbes, The Elements of Law, ed. Ferdinand Toennies (Cambridge, 1928), p. 93. This book is edited from MSS. of Human Nature and De Corpore Politico which were published in 1650.
[113]   Hobbes, Leviathan (Ch. 13), p. 84.
[114]   Hobbes, Leviathan (Ch. 17), pp. 115-19.
[115]   Hobbes, Leviathan (Ch. 39), p. 342.
[116]   Collingwood, The Idea of Nature, pp. 5, 95, 103. Hobbes' difficulties in applying Galileo's scientific method to political philosophy are discussed by Leo Strauss, The Political Philosophy of Thomas Hobbes, trans. Elsa M. Sinclair (Chicago, 1952), pp. 6-7.

series of comparisons between the parts of a human body and "Engines that move themselves by springs and wheeles as doth a watch": the heart is a spring, the nerves are strings, and "the *Joynts*, but so many *Wheeles*".[117] The state possesses no inherent order, but only such order as is imposed upon it by man.

Neither priest nor presbyter regarded Hobbes with any affection.[118] Yet by defining the Leviathan as a body politic and artificial, Hobbes established the frame of reference for future political controversies. Moreover, Hobbes, Milton, and the Levellers combined to put an end to sustained or serious use of organic imagery in political discussion by pamphleteers or poets. The idea of a social contract, whatever its validity or utility, appeals exclusively to the argumentative reason, not to the poetic imagination.

---

[117]   Hobbes, *Leviathan*, p. xviii.
[118]   A general survey is Samuel I. Mintz, *The Hunting of Leviathan: Seventeenth-Century Reactions to the Materialism and Moral Philosophy of Thomas Hobbes* (Cambridge, 1962).

VI

EPILOGUE

Although the idea of a body politic had lost most of its validity by the middle of the seventeenth century, the analogy between organism and society did not suddenly disappear from the rhetorical resources of the English language. With the general acceptance of Lockean politics and Newtonian physics, a serious acceptance of the concept of an organic society was difficult if not impossible. But the analogy continued to be used. These applications were brief, unoriginal, and void of any implications rising from the analogy. In the nineteenth century the development of evolutionary biology contributed both language and ideas to the discussion of politics and the historical study of political institutions. In the twentieth century there is frequent use of the phrase 'body politic' as a synonym for 'nation'. Relatively 'literary' writers avoid it; there also seem to be in process further revisions of the scientific attitudes which underlie the possible validity of the metaphor. These few concluding pages survey a few examples from the three centuries since the publication of *Leviathan*.

In Dryden's *The Indian Emperor* (1667) there is an interesting exchange between Alibech and Guyomar as she attempts to defend her betrayal of Montezuma:

> *Alib.* When kings grow stubborn, slothful, or unwise,
> Each private man for public good should rise.
> As when the head distempers does endure.
> Each part must join to effect the cure.
> *Guy.* Take heed, fair maid, how monarchs you accuse:
> Such reasons none but impious rebels use. . . .[1]

Guyomar then proceeds with a little lecture about kingship and the duties of passive obedience.

The fable of the belly continued to appear in editions of Aesop

---

[1] John Dryden, *The Indian Emperor*, IV.ii.73-78, in: *The Dramatic Works of John Dryden*, ed. George Saintsbury, 8 vols. (Edinburgh, 1882), II, 377.

which flowed from the presses; these were mostly intended for use in schools and were usually reprints or revisions of earlier texts. The important version by Sir Roger L'Estrange (1692) is unique in its fusion of several traditions. The Aesopic fable is connected to Menenius and the plebeian revolt. The moral of the fable moves the center of authority from the belly to the head: *"The Publick is but One Body, and the Prince the Head on't; so that what Member soever withdraws his Service from the Head, is no Better than a Negative Traitor to his Country."* There follows a long "Reflexion" on the "allegory", which in part says that "There is so Near an *Analogy* betwixt the State of a Body Natural, and Politique, that the Necessity of Government and Obedience cannot be better Represented".[2] A comparison for the purpose of argument is not, however, an identity.

Lord Chesterfield wrote a brief history of Rome in a series of letters to his very young son. Emphasizing the development of "un gouvernement libre", he recounted the plebeian secession to the Mons Sacer and Menenius' fable which, with the establishment of the tribuneship, reconciled the people.[3] In *Spectator* No. 174 Steele mentions "the Sedition of the Members of the human Body in the old *Roman* Fable" as an example of the necessity of agreement between the conflicting parties represented by Sir Roger de Coverly and Sir Andrew Freeport.[4]

Also in the eighteenth century two more specifically political examples may be mentioned. About 1750 the Prince of Wales commissioned one Henry McCulloh to prepare a series of reports on the efficiency of the British government. Urging reform, McCulloh introduced one of his reports by writing:

It has been often Observed that the politick as well as the natural Body is liable to many Disorders, & as in the Natural Body they take their Rise in the Blood, so in the Politick they often taken their Rise from the undue Circulation of Business in the publick Boards. . . .[5]

If business is free, kingdoms will be healthy; but if there is too much official interference, they will be sick "if not nigh unto death". That

---

[2]   Roger L'Estrange, *Fables of Aesop and other Eminent Mythologists* (London, 1692), pp. 50, 51.
[3]   Lord Chesterfield, Letter XXI, *The Letters of Philip Dormer Stanhope 4th Earl of Chesterfield*, ed. Bonamy Dobrée, 6 vols. (London, 1932), II, 353.
[4]   *The Spectator*, ed. G. Gregory Smith, 4 vols., Everyman's Library (London & New York, 1907), II, 20.
[5]   Henry McCulloh, "A Treatise endeavouring to Demonstrate . . .", fol. 13r-v. MS. in the McCulloh Papers, Duke University Library. I am grateful to Mr. William R. Erwin for calling this document to my attention. Cf. Swift, *Gulliver's Travels*, III, 6.

old conservative, Dr. Johnson, turned the analogy against the claims of the colonists in America:

A colony is to the mother-country, as a member to the body, deriving its action and its strength from the general principle of vitality; receiving from the body, and communicating to it, all the benefits and evils of health and disease; liable, in dangerous maladies, to sharp applications, of which the body, however, must partake in pain; and exposed, if incurably tainted, to amputation, by which the body, likewise, will be mutilated.[6]

Should the colonies separate from England, they will perish like amputated limbs. Johnson's sentences contain an uncommon amount of detail, but again their important aspect is a concern for administration and economics as the unifying, vital factors.

Dr. Johnson wrote in vain; the day was carried by the descendants of the Puritans, who expressed themselves in terms which echo those of the Mayflower Compact: "The body politic is formed by a voluntary association of individuals: it is a social compact, by which the whole people covenants with each citizen, and each citizen with the whole people, that all shall be governed by certain laws for the common good."[7] A similar fusion of organism and contract is found in Rousseau's *Du Contrat Social* (1762) but with an important difference; Rousseau is striving, searching for an unrealized, emotional relationship to society.

Rousseau's alienation from the present is a part of romanticism's turning to the past, especially to the Middle Ages. Hence there is a greater tendency for social criticism to be expressed through organic imagery. Southey envoked the ghost of Sir Thomas More to castigate the manufacturing system: "It is a wen, a fungous excrescence from the body politic: the growth ... has acquired so great a bulk, its nerves have branched so widely ... that to remove it by absorption is impossible, and excision would be fatal."[8] Montesinos' response to this is, "Happily, this is but a metaphor; and the body politic, like its crowned head, never dies." England and its king are immortal corporations, legal fictions. But this concept of a legal fiction was, according to Jeremy Bentham, a grievous flaw in the English legal system, "a *syphilis*, which

---

[6]   Samuel Johnson, *Taxation No Tyranny* (1775), in: *The Complete Works of Samuel Johnson*, 8 vols. (Cambridge, Mass., n.d.), VII, 109.
[7]   "Preamble", *Constitution of the Commonwealth of Massachusetts* (Boston, 1927), p. 3.
[8]   Robert Southey, *Sir Thomas More*, 2 vols. (London, 1829), I, 171.

runs in every vein, and carries into every part of the system the principle of rottenness".[9]

A more sweeping indictment of contemporary England is found in the works of Thomas Carlyle. Appalled by the Industrial Revolution and its byproducts – Mammonism, utilitarianism, and the degradation of the workers – and by the futility of efforts at reform, Carlyle urged a national rebirth in spirit which would produce unity and security similar to the emotional comforts provided by feudalism. The metaphor of the body politic first appears in *Sartor Resartus* (1836):

> For if Government is, so to speak, the outward SKIN of the Body Politic, holding the whole together and protecting it; and all your Craft-Guilds, and Associations for Industry, of hand or of head, are the Fleshly Clothes, the muscular and osseous Tissues (lying *under* such SKIN), whereby Society stands and works; – then is Religion the inmost Pericardial and Nervous Tissue, which ministers Life and warm Circulation to the whole. Without which Pericardial Tissue the Bones and Muscles (of Industry) were inert, or animated only by a Galvanic vitality; the SKIN would become a shrivelled pelt, or fast-rotting rawhide; and Society itself a dead carcass, – deserving to be buried.[10]

But Religion has lost its efficacy; England lies "in sick discontent, writhing powerless on its fever-bed . . .".[11] Discontent among the lower classes produces an impulse for reform or repression. But for Carlyle, "Glasgow Thuggery, Chartist torch-meetings, Birmingham riots, Swing conflagrations, are so many symptoms on the surface; you abolish the symptom to no purpose, if the disease is left untouched."[12] This disease afflicts the heart, the soul of the body politic. Mechanism, laissez-faire capitalism, and utilitarianism have destroyed the vital interdependency of man; "this is verily the plague spot; center of the universal Social Gangrene, threatening all modern things with frightful death."[13]

England needs "A total change of regimen, change of constitution and existence from the very centre of it; a new body to be got, with resuscitated soul . . .".[14] To portray the difference between the un-

---

[9]   Jeremy Bentham, *The Elements of the Art of Packing as applied to Special Juries* (1821), in: *The Works of Jeremy Bentham*, ed. John Bowring, 11 vols. (New York, 1962), V, 92.

[10]   Thomas Carlyle, *Sartor Resartus*, in: *The Complete Works of Thomas Carlyle*, 30 vols. (London, 1896-99), I, 172. See Frederick W. Roe, *The Social Philosophy of Carlyle and Ruskin* (New York, 1921).

[11]   Carlyle, "Chartism" (1840), *Works*, XXIX, 129.

[12]   Carlyle, "Chartism", *Works*, XXIX, 120.

[13]   Carlyle, *Past and Present* (1843), *Works*, X, 137.

[14]   Carlyle, *Past and Present, Works*, X, 36.

happy now and a happier then, Carlyle devotes much of *Past and Present* to recreating life in St. Edmundsbury monastery under the benign administration of Abbot Samson in the twelfth century. Men were aware of their responsibilities and obligations; most of the time they tried to fulfill them. Moreover, Gurth the swineherd had "the inexpressible satisfaction of feeling himself related indissolubly, though in a rude brass-collar way, to his fellow-mortals in this Earth".[15] Society was an organic whole, not a conglomeration of bits of inert matter. Carlyle proposes that a religious, though not specifically Christian, revival take the form of an increase of hero-worship: "we must learn to do our Hero-worship better; that to do it better and better, means the awakening of the Nation's soul from its asphyxia, and the return of blessed life to us, – Heaven's blessed life, not Mammon's galvanic accursed one."[16] But Carlylean hero-worship is not really very medieval; it is not a reciprocal relationship and is, paradoxically, a product of the individualism of the Reformation, of Carlyle's Calvinistic heritage.

A new development in the history of the organic analogy was the application of biological evolution to the study of politics.[17] One of the best known examples is the work of Herbert Spencer, especially *The Principles of Sociology*. This book is as full of comparisons between natural and politic bodies as John of Salisbury's *Policraticus* or Starkey's *Dialogue*, indeed more so. There are, however, a number of important differences. Spencer availed himself of a wider and more sophisticated fund of information about the varieties of living beings and social organizations; the scope of his work is consequently much larger. Instead of likening the commonwealth or England to a man's body, he can compare a small, primitive tribe to a simple form of life and a large, industrialized nation to a highly complex organism. Man, therefore, is not the only microcosm, is not really a microcosm at all. Man and society do not correspond to each other, but are both living organisms between whom a number of important similarities exist.

Describing societies in terms of a variety of organisms facilitates the discussion of growth and evolution. "It is a character of social bodies, as of living bodies, that while they increase in size they increase in

---

15   Carlyle, *Past and Present, Works*, X, 212.
16   Carlyle, *Past and Present, Works*, X, 34-35.
17   An introductory survey of the nineteenth century is Francis W. Coker, *Organismic Theories of the State: Nineteenth Century Interpretations of the State as Organism or as Person*, Columbia University Studies in History, Economics, and Public Law No. 101 (New York, 1910).

structure."[18] An increasingly large society evolves a more complex
structure; various parts perform specialized functions – the division of
labor described in Plato's *Republic*. Spencer analyzes the parts of a
society, their structure and operation, in elaborate detail; the liver and
the factory system are compared at length.[19] Newspapers are like nerves.
He does not, however, produce a neat set of correspondences in the
medieval tradition; such correspondences had been out of date since
the seventeenth-century recognition that the static, medieval ideal of an
ordered hierarchy was out of touch with reality.[20]

In the twentieth century the analogy seems to have lost much of its
appeal. The phrase "body politic" appears often and writers are not un-
willing to say that the body politic is diseased. More extensive comparisons are very rare. One example is found in Shaw's *Saint Joan* as
Cauchon lectures Warwick about heresy:

[*Cauchon*.]   It is cancerous: if it be not cut out, stamped out, burnt out, it
will not stop until it has brought the whole body of human society into sin
and corruption, into waste and ruin.[21]

More interesting, however, are certain developments in the philosophy of science. Bacon and his followers abandoned the idea of microcosm and macrocosm because there was no substantiating empirical
evidence. Professor Conger of the University of Minnesota has surveyed
a wide field of recent scientific findings and uses this information to
support the thesis that:

The universe ... presents itself as a vast system of systems which are strik-
ingly similar in the general principles of their structures and processes. ...
The resemblances of structures and processes throughout the levels and
realms indicate that the universe is not merely a series of evolutions, but
also of 'epitomizations' and 'cumulative coordinations'.[22]

He quotes with approval a statement by Dr. Walter P. Cannon that
"The analogies between the body physiological and the body politic are
so close and so numerous as to suggest that there are, indeed, general

[18]   Herbert Spencer, *The Principles of Sociology*, 3rd ed., 3 vols. (New York, 1897),
I, 449. Spencer's work is summarized in Coker, *Organismic Theories of the State*;
pp. 124-39.
[19]   Spencer, *The Principles of Sociology*, I, 482.
[20]   See Ruth Mohl, *The Three Estates in Medieval and Renaissance Literature*,
Columbia University Studies in English and Comparative Literature No. 114 (New
York, 1933), p. 383.
[21]   G. Bernard Shaw, *Saint Joan* (Sc. iv) in *The Collected Writings of Bernard
Shaw*, 30 vols. (New York, 1930), XVII, 103.
[22]   George P. Conger, *Synoptic Naturalism* (Minneapolis, 1960), p. vi.

principles of organization widely applicable to complex aggregations of collaborating parts".[23] In an earlier essay Cannon wrote that the closest analogue is the system of production and distribution of merchandise in both kinds of bodies.[24] The continuing influence of Herbert Spencer is clear.

The problems which agitated the English Renaissance are still with us, albeit in other forms. And though our thinking about these problems is, often, still in myths and metaphors, much has changed. Menenius Agrippa can no longer bring a city to good order with a pretty fable; it is a mere trope of rhetoric to describe a group of tradesmen as serving the function of an organ of the human body. Our understanding of the nature of man and his relation to his fellows is complex and fragmented. The imagery of the body politic no longer delights and instructs, no longer holds the mirror up to nature. To lament this change may be futile; to recognize it, imperative.

[23] Walter P. Cannon in *Scientific Monthly*, quoted in Conger, *Synoptic Naturalism*, p. 240. Cannon was professor of physiology at Harvard Medical School.
[24] Walter P. Cannon, "The Body Physiologic and the Body Politic", in *Science and Man*, ed. Ruth N. Anshen (New York, 1942), p. 296. More recently, Norman O. Brown has argued for a return to this earlier form of human consciousness. Many of the texts discussed above are re-examined from a Freudian point of view, sometimes producing distorted conclusions (*Love's Body* [New York, 1966]).

BIBLIOGRAPHY

Aesop, *Aesop Without Morals*, trans. Lloyd W. Daly (New York & London, 1961).
——, *Aesopica*, ed. Ben E. Perry (Urbana, Ill., 1952).
——, *Fables of Aesop and other Eminent Mythologists*, trans. Roger L'Estrange (London, 1692).
——, *The Fables of Aesop, as first printed by William Caxton*, ed. Joseph Jacobs, 2 vols. (London, 1889).
——, *The Fables of Aesop*, trans. W. Barret (London, 1639).
——, *Fabulae versibus descriptae*, ed. Humphrey Roydon (London, 1596).
——, *Lyoner Yzopet*, ed. Wendelin Foerster (Altfranzoesische Bibliothek V. Heilbronn, 1882).
——, *Ysopet-Avionnet*, ed. Kenneth McKenzie and William A. Oldfather (*University of Illinois Studies in Language and Literature* V) (Urbana, Ill., 1919).
Allen, J. W., *English Political Thought: 1603-1644* (London, 1938).
——, *A History of Political Thought in the Sixteenth Century* (London, 1938).
Allers, Rudolf, "Microcosmus: From Anaximandros to Paracelsus", *Traditio*, II (1944), 319-407.
Ancrene Riwle, English Text, ed. Mable Day, EETS, O. S. 225 (London, 1952).
Anderson, F. H., *The Philosophy of Francis Bacon* (Chicago, 1948).
Aquinas, Thomas, *Summa Theologica*, trans. Fathers of English Dominican Province, 3 vols. (New York, 1947).
The Apostolic Fathers, trans. Kirsopp Lake. 2 vols (= *Loeb Library*) (London & New York, 1912-13).
Archambault, Paul, "The Analogy of the 'Body' in Renaissance Political Literature", *Bibliothèque d'Humanisme et Renaissance*, XXIX (1967), 21-53.
Aristophanes, trans. Benjamin B. Rogers, 3 vols. (= *Loeb Library*) (London & New York, 1924).
Aristotle, *On the Movement of Animals*, trans. E. S. Forster (= *Loeb Library*) (Cambridge, Mass., & London, 1937).
——, *The Politics*, trans. Benjamin Jowett, 2 vols. (Oxford, 1885).
Augustine, *The City of God*, trans. Marcus Dods (New York, 1950).
Averell, William, *A Mervailous Combat of Contrarieties* (London, 1588).
Bacon, Francis, *The Advancement of Learning*, ed. William A. Wright, 5th ed. (Oxford, 1900).
——, *A Harmony of the Essays*, ed. Edward Arber (London, 1871).
——, *The Moral and Historical Works of Lord Bacon*, ed. Joseph Devey (= *Bohn's Library*) (London, 1909).
——, *The Physical and Metaphysical Works of Lord Bacon*, ed. Joseph Devey (= *Bohn's Library*) (London, 1911).
Barker, Ernest, *Greek Political Theory: Plato and His Predecessors*, 2nd ed. (London, 1925).

Barlow, William, *The First of the foure Sermons Preached before the Kings Majestie* (London, 1607).

Barnes, Barnabe, *Foure Bookes of Offices* (London, 1606).

Basil, *The Letters of St. Basil*, trans. Roy J. Deferrari, 4 vols. (= *Loeb Library*) London & New York, 1926-34).

Baumer, Franklin LeV., *The Early Tudor Theory of Kingship* (New Haven, 1940).

——, "Thomas Starkey and Marsilius of Padua", *Politica*, II (1936), 188-205.

Beaumont, Francis, and John Fletcher, *The Works of Francis Beaumont and John Fletcher*, ed. Arnold Glover and A. R. Waller, 10 vols. (Cambridge, 1905-12).

Bentham, Jeremy, *The Works of Jeremy Bentham*, ed. John Browning, 11 vols. (New York, 1962).

Boas, F. S., *"Macbeth* and *Lingua"*, *Modern Language Review*, IV (1909), 517-20.

Bock, Hellmut, *Staat und Gesellschaft bei Francis Bacon* (Berlin, 1937).

Bodin, Jean, *The Six Bookes of a Commonweale*, trans. Richard Knolles (London, 1606).

The Book of Sir Thomas More, ed. Walter W. Greg, Malone Society (Oxford, 1911).

Bradford, William, *Of Plymouth Plantation: 1620-1647*, ed. Samuel E. Morison (New York, 1952).

Bradley, A. C., "Coriolanus", *Proceedings of the British Academy*, V (1912), 457-74.

Breton, Nicholas, *The Works in Verse and Prose*, ed. Alexander B. Grosart, 2 vols. (= *Chertsey Worthies' Library*) (Edinburgh) 1875-79.

Brinton, Thomas, *The Sermons of Thomas Brinton, Bishop of Rochester*, ed. Sister Mary Aquinas Devlin, 2 vols. Camden Society, 3rd ser., LXXXVI (London, 1954).

Brooke, Stopford A., *On Ten Plays of Shakespeare* (New York, 1905).

Brown, Norman O., *Love's Body* (New York, 1966).

Browne, Robert, *A Booke which Sheweth the life and manners of all true christians* (Middelburgh, 1582).

Browne, Thomas, *Religio Medici*, ed. Jean-Jacques Denonain (Cambridge, 1953).

Burton, Robert, *The Anatomy of Melancholy*, ed. A. R. Shilleto, 3 vols. (London, 1896).

Bush, Douglas, *English Literature in the Earlier Seventeenth Century: 1600-1660*, 2nd ed. (Oxford, 1962).

Calvin, John, *A Commentarie upon S. Pauls Epistle to the Corinthians*, trans. Thomas Timme (London, 1577).

——, *Institutes of the Christian Religion*, trans. Ford L. Battles, 2 vols. (= *The Library of Christian Classics*) (Philadelphia, 1960).

Camden, William, *Remaines of a greater worke concerning Britaine* (London, 1605).

Campbell, Oscar J., *Shakespeare's Satire* (New York) 1943.

Cannon, Walter P., "The Body Physiologic and the Body Politic", in *Science and Man*, ed. Ruth N. Anshen (New York, 1942).

Carew, Thomas, *The Poems of Thomas Carew*, ed. Rhodes Dunlap (Oxford, 1949).

Carlyle, R. W., and A. J., *A History of Mediaeval Political Theory in the West*, 6 vols (Edinburgh & London, 1903-36).

Carlyle, Thomas, *The Complete Works of Thomas Carlyle*, 30 vols. (London, 1896-99).

Carrol, Sister M. Thomas, *The Venerable Bede: His Spiritual Teachings* (= *Catholic University of America Studies in Medieval History N. S. IX*) (Washington, D.C., 1946).

Caspari, Fritz, *Humanism and the Social Order in Tudor England* (Chicago, 1954).
Caxton's Aesop, ed. R. T. Lenaghan (Cambridge, Mass., 1967).
Certayne Sermons, or Homilies (London, 1547).
Charney, Maurice, *Shakespeare's Roman Plays* (Cambridge, Mass., 1961).
Cheke, John, *The Hurt of Sedition, how grievous it is to a common welth* (London, 1549).
Chelidonius Tigurinus, *Of the Institution and first beginning of Christian Princes, and of the Original of Kingdomes*, trans. James Chillester (London, 1571).
Chesterfield, The Earl of, *The Letters of Philip Dormer Stanhope 4th Earl of Chesterfield*, ed. Bonamy Dobrée, 6 vols. (London, 1932).
Chrimes, S. B., *English Constitutional Ideas in the Fifteenth Century* (Cambridge, 1936).
——, "Sir John Fortescue and his Theory of Dominion", *Transactions of the Royal Historical Society*, 4th ser., XVII (1934), 117-47.
Chroust, Anton-Hermann, "The Corporate Idea and the Body Politic in the Middle Ages", *The Review of Politics*, IX (1947), 423-52.
Clayton, A. C., *The Rig-Veda and Vedic Religion* (London & Madras, 1913).
Coker, Francis W., *Organismic Theories of the State: Nineteenth Century Interpretations of the State as Organism or as Person* (= *Columbia University Studies in History, Economics and Public Law* No. 101) (New York, 1910).
Coleridge, Samuel T., *Coleridge's Shakespearean Criticism*, ed. Thomas M. Raysor, 2 vols. (London, 1930).
Collingwood, R. G., *The Idea of Nature* (Oxford, 1945).
Conger, George P., "Cosmic Persons and Human Universes in Indian Philosophy", *Journal of the Asiatic Society of Bengal*, N. S. XXIX (1933), 255-70.
——, *Synoptic Naturalism* (Minneapolis, 1960).
——, *Theories of Macrocosms and Microcosms in the History of Philosophy* (New York, 1922).
Constitution of the Commonwealth of Massachusetts (Boston, 1927).
Craig, Thomas, *Concerning the Right of Succession to the Kingdom of England*, trans. J. G. (London, 1703).
Crowley, Robert, *The Select Works of Robert Crowley*, ed. J. M. Cowper, EETS, E. S. 15 (London, 1872).
Daniel, Samuel, *The Civil Wars*, ed. Laurence Michel (New Haven, 1958).
——, *Poems and "A Defence of Ryme"*, ed. Arthur C. Sprague (Cambridge, Mass., 1930).
Davies, Godfrey, *The Early Stuarts: 1603-1660*, 2nd ed. (Oxford, 1959).
De Coulanges, Fustel, *The Ancient City*, trans. Willard Small (Garden City, N.Y., 1956).
Dekker, Thomas, *The Dramatic Works of Thomas Dekker*, ed. Fredson Bowers, 5 vols. (Cambridge, 1953-).
——, *The Non-Dramtic Works of Thomas Dekker*, ed. Alexander B. Grosart, 5 vols. (London, 1884-86).
Demosthenes, *The Olynthiac and Other Public Orations*, trans. Charles R. Kennedy (= *Bohn's Library*) (London, 1865).
Dickinson, John, "The Mediaeval Conception of Kingship as Developed in the *Politcraticus* of John of Salisbury", *Speculum*, I (1926), 307-37.
Dio Cocceianus, *Roman History*, trans. Earnest Cary, 9 vols. (= *Loeb Library*) (London & New York, 1914-27).
Dionysius of Halicarnassus, *Roman Antiquities*, trans. Earnest Cary, 7 vols. (= *Loeb Library*) *(London & New York, 1937-50)*.
Dodsley's Old English Plays, ed. W. Carew Hazlitt, 4th ed. 8 vols. (London, 1874).
Donne, John, *John Donne: The Anniversaries*, ed. Frank Manly (Baltimore, 1963).

Dowden, Edward, *Shakespeare: His Mind and Art* (New York, 1905).

Draper, John W., "Political Themes in Shakespeare's Later Plays", *Journal of English and Germanic Philology*, XXXV (1936), 61-93.

Drayton, Michael, *The Works of Michael Drayton*, ed. J. William Hebel, 5 vols. (Oxford, 1931-41).

Dryden, John, *The Dramatic Works of John Dryden*, ed. George Saintsbury, 8 vols. (Edinburgh, 1882).

Eikon Basilike, ed. Edward J. L. Scott (London, 1880).

Elyot, Thomas, *The Boke Named the Governour*, ed. Henry H. S. Croft, 2 vols. (London,1880).

Emerson, Everett H., "Calvin and Covenant Theology", *Church History*, XXV (1956), 136-44.

Farmer, Richard, *A Sermon Preached at Pauls Crosse* (London, 1629).

Farnham, Willard, *Shakespeare's Tragic Frontiers* (Berkeley & Los Angeles, 1950).

Ferguson, Arthur B., "Fortescue and the Renaissance: A Study in Transition", *Studies in the Renaissance*, VI (1959), 175-94.

——, "Renaissance Realism in the 'Commonwealth' Literature of Early Tudor England", *Journal of the History of Ideas*, XVI (1955), 287-305.

——, "The Tudor Commonweal and the Sense of Change", *The Journal of British Studies*, III (1963), 11-35.

Ferne, Henry, *The Resolving of Conscience upon this Question* (Cambridge, 1642).

Figgis, J. Neville, *The Divine Right of Kings*, 2nd ed. (Cambridge, 1922).

——, *The Political Aspects of S. Augustine's "City of God"* (London, 1921).

——, *Political Thought from Gerson to Grotius*, 2nd ed. (Cambridge, 1916).

Fink, Zera S., *The Classical Republicans* (= *Northwestern University Studies in the Humanities* No. 9) (Evanston, Ill., 1945).

Fisher, John, *The English Works of John Fisher*, ed. John E. B. Mayor, EETS, E. S. 27 (London, 1876).

Floyd, Thomas, *The Picture of a perfit Common wealth* (London, 1600).

Ford, John, *The Works of John Ford*, ed. Alexander Dyce, 3 vols. (London, 1869).

Forset, Edward, *A Comparative Discourse of the Bodies Natural and Politic* (London, 1606).

——, *A Defense of the Right of Kings* (London, 1624).

Fortescue, John, *De Laudibus Legum Anglie*, trans. S. B. Chrimes (Cambridge, 1942).

Fuller, Thomas, *The Holy State and the Profane State*, ed. Maximilian G. Walten, 2 vols. (= *Columbia University Studies in English and Comparative Literature* No. 136) (New York, 1938).

Furnivall, F. J., "Sir John Harrington's Shakespeare Quartos", *Notes and Queries*, 7th ser. IX (1890), 382-83.

Gardiner, Stephen, *Obedience in Church & State*, ed. and trans. Pierre Janelle (Cambridge, 1930).

Gee, John A., *The Life and Works of Thomas Lupset* (New Haven, 1928).

Gewirth, Alan, *Marsilus of Padua: The Defender of Peace*, 2 vols. (New York, 1956).

Gierke, Otto, *Natural Law and the Theory of Society*, trans. Ernest Barker, 2 vols. (Cambridge, 1934).

——, *Political Theories of the Middle Age*, trans. Frederic W. Maitland (Cambridge, 1900).

Gilbert, Felix, "Sir John Fortescue's *Dominium Regale et Politicum*", *Medievalia et Humanistica*, II (1944), 87-97.

Gombel, Heinrich, "Die Fabel 'Vom Magen und den Gliedern' in der Weltliteratur", *Beihefte zur Zeitschrift für Romanische Philologie*, Heft 80 (Halle, 1934).

Gough, J. W., *The Social Contract*, 2nd ed. (Oxford, 1957).

Greene, Robert, *The Second Part of Cony-Catching*, ed. G. B. Harrison (London, 1923).

Haller, William, *Liberty and Reformation in the Puritan Revolution* (New York, 1955).

——, *The Rise of Puritanism* (New York, 1938).

——, ed. *Tracts on Liberty in the Puritan Revolution: 1638-1647*, 3 vols. (New York, 1934).

——, and Godfrey Davies, eds., *The Leveller Tracts: 1647-1653* (New York, 1944).

Hardy, Alexandre, *Le Theatre d'Alexandre Hardy*, ed. E. Stengel, 5 vols. (Marburg, 1884).

Hart, Alfred, *Shakespeare and the Homilies* (Melburne, 1934).

Hazlitt, William, *The Characters of Shakespeare's Plays* (London, 1907).

Hearnshaw, F. J. C., ed. *The Social and Political Ideas of Some Great Medieval Thinkers* (London, 1923).

——, *The Social and Political Ideas of Some Great Thinkers of the Renaissance and Reformation* (London, 1925).

——, *The Social and Political Ideas of Some Great Thinkers of the Sixteenth and Seventeenth Centuries* (London, 1926).

Henderson, Ernest F., trans. *Select Historical Documents of the Middle Ages* (London, 1896).

Heninger, S. K., Jr. "The Sun-King Analogy in *Richard II*", *Shakespeare Quarterly*, XI (1960), 319-27.

Henry VIII, *A copy of the letter wherin ... Henry the eight made answere unto a certeyn letter of Martyn Luther* (London, n. d.).

Hervieux, Léopold, *Les Fabulists Latins*, 5 vols. (Paris, 1884-99 rpr. New York, 1964).

Hill, R. P., "Coriolanus: Violentest Contrariety", *Essays and Studies*, N. S. XVII (1964), 12-23.

Hinton, R. W. K., "English Constitutional Theories: Sir John Fortescue to Sir John Eliot", *English Historical Review*, LXXV (1960), 410-25.

Hobbes, Thomas, *The Elements of Law: Natural & Politic*, ed. Ferdinand Toennies (Cambridge, 1928).

——, *Leviathan*, ed. A. R. Waller, (Cambridge, 1904).

Hofling, Charles K., "An Interpretation of Shakespeare's *Coriolanus*," *American Image*, XIV (1957), 407-35.

An Homily agaynst disobedience and wylful rebellion (London, 1570).

Hooker, Richard, *The Works of Mr. Richard Hooker*, ed. John Keble, 3 vols. 7th ed. (Oxford, 1888).

Howell, James, *England's Teares, For the Present Wars* (London, 1644).

Hudson, Winthrop S., *John Ponet: Advocate of Limited Monarchy* (Chicago, 1942).

Isocrates, trans. George Norlin and Larue Van Hook, 3 vols. (= *Loeb Library*) (London & New York, 1929-45).

Jacob, E. F., "Sir John Fortescue and the Law of Nature", *Bulletin of the John Rylands Library*, XVIII (1934), 359-76.

James I., *The Political Works of James I*, ed. C. H. McIlwain (Cambridge, Mass., 1918).

——, *A Royal Rhetorician*, ed. Robert S. Rait (New York, 1900).

John of Salisbury, *The Statesman's Book*, trans. John Dickinson (New York, 1927).

Johnson, Samuel, *The Complete Works of Samuel Johnson*, 8 vols. (Cambridge, Mass., n. d.).

Jones-Davies, M. T., *Un Peintre de la Vie Londonienne: Thomas Dekker*, 2 vols. (Paris, 1958).

Kail, J., ed., *Twenty-Six Political and Other Poems*, EETS, O. S. 124 (London, 1904).

Kantorowicz, Ernst H., *The King's Two Bodies: A Study in Mediaeval Political Theology* (Princeton, 1957).

Kern, Fritz, *Kingship and Law in the Middle Ages*, trans. S. B. Chrimes (Cambridge, 1939).

Kitto, H. D. F., *The Greeks* (Harmondsworth, 1951).

Knappen, M. M., *Tudor Puritanism* (Chicago, 1939).

Knox, John, *The History of the Reformation of Religion in Scotland*, ed. Cuthbert Lennox (London, 1905).

Latimer, Hugh, *Sermons*, ed. George E. Corrie, 2 vols. Parker Society (Cambridge, 1844).

Laski, Harold J., *The Foundations of Sovereignty and Other Essays* (New York, 1921).

Laud, William, *The Works of Archbishop Laud*, ed. William Scott, 9 vols. (= Library of Anglo-Catholic Theology) (Oxford, 1847-57).

Lees, F. N., "*Coriolanus*, Aristotle, and Bacon", *Review of English Studies*, N. S. I. (1950), 114-25).

Levi, Adolpho, *Il Pensiero di Francesco Bacone* (Turin, 1925).

Lewis, C. S., *The Discarded Image: An Introduction to Medieval and Renaissance Literature* (Cambridge, 1964).

Lewis, Ewart, "Organic Tendencies in Medieval Political Thought", *American Political Science Review*, XXXII (1938), 849-76.

Liebeschuetz, H., "John of Salisbury and the Pseudo-Plutarch", *Journal of the Warburg and Courtauld Institutes*, VI (1943), 33-39.

Livy, trans. B. O. Foster, 14 vols. (= *Loeb Library*) (London & New York, 1919-59).

Lloyd, Lodowik, *The Stratgems of Jerusalem* (London, 1602).

Lovejoy, Arthur O., *The Great Chain of Being* (Cambridge, Mass., 1936).

Lovelace, Richard, *The Poems of Richard Lovelace*, ed. C. H. Wilkinson (Oxford, 1930).

Lubac, Henri de, *Corpus Mysticum: L'Eucharistie et L'Eglise au Moyen Age*, 2nd ed. (Paris, 1949).

Lydgate, John, *The Fall of Princes*, ed. Henry Bergen, EETS E. S. 121 (London, 1924).

Lyly, John, *The Complete Works of John Lyly*, ed. R. Warwick Bond, 3 vols. (Oxford, 1902).

MacCallum, M. W., *Shakespeare's Roman Plays and their Background* (London, 1910).

McCulloh, Henry, "A Treatise endeavouring to Demonstrate, . . ." MS. Duke University Library.

McDavid, Raven I., "Milton as a Political Thinker", unpublished dissertation, Duke University, 1935.

The Mahabharata, trans. Manmatha N. Dutt., 14 vols. (Calcutta, 1905).

Maitland, F. W., *Selected Esays,* ed. H. D. Hazeltine, *et al.* (Cambridge, 1936).

Mall, E. "Zur Geschichte der mittelalterlichen Fabellitteratur und insbesondere des Esope der Marie der France", *Zeitschrift für Romanische Philologie*, IX (1885), 161-203.

Marprelate, Martin, *Hay any worke for Cooper* (N.p., 1589).

Marston, John, *The Plays of John Marston*, ed. H. Harvey Wood, 3 vols. (Edinburgh & London, 1934-39).

144 BIBLIOGRAPHY

Martin Junior, *Theses Martinianae* (N.p., 1589).

Maxwell, J. C. "Animal Imagery in *Coriolanus*", *Modern Language Review*, XLII (1947), 417-21.

Mazzeo, Joseph A., "Universal Analogy and the Culture of the Renaissance", *Journal of the History of Ideas*, XV (1954) 299-304.

Michel of Northgate, *Ayenbite of Inwyt*, ed. Richard Morris, EETS, O. S. 23 (London, 1866).

Middleton, Thomas, *The Works of Thomas Middleton*, ed. A. H. Bullen, 8 vols. (London, 1885-86).

Miles, Leland, *John Colet and the Platonic Tradition* (La Salle, Ill.) 1961.

Miller, Perry, *Errand into the Wilderness* (Cambridge, Mass., 1956).

Milton, John, *Complete Prose Works of John Milton*, gen. ed. Don M. Wolfe, 8 vols. (New Haven, 1953-).

——, *The Works of John Milton*, gen. ed. Frank A. Patterson, 18 vols. (New York, 1931-38).

Mintz, Samuel I., *The Hunting of Leviathan; Seventeenth-Century Reactions to the Materialism and Moral Philosophy of Thomas Hobbes* (Cambridge, 1962).

Mohl, Ruth, *The Three Estates in Medieval and Renaissance Literature* (= Columbia University Studies in English and Comparative Literature No. 114) (New York, 1933).

More, Thomas, *The Apologye of Syr Thomas More, Knyght*, ed. Arthur I. Taft, EETS, O. S. 180 (London, 1930).

——, *The Correspondence of Sir Thomas More*, ed. Elizabeth F. Rogers (Princeton, 1947).

——, *The Dialogue Concerning Tyndale*, ed. W. E. Campbell (London, 1927).

——, *The Latin Epigrams of Thomas More*, ed. and trans. Leicester Bradner and Charles A. Lynch (Chicago, 1953).

Morison, Richard, *An Exhortation to styre all Englyshe men to the defense of theyr countrye* (London, 1539).

Morley, Henry, ed. *Character Writings of the Seventeenth Century* (London, 1891).

Mueller, William R., *The Anatomy of Robert Burton's England* (= University of California Publications in English Studies No. 2.) (Berkeley & Los Angeles, 1952).

Muir, Kenneth, "Menenius's Fable", *Notes and Queries*, CXCVIII (1953), 240-42.

Murray, R. H., *The Political Consequences of the Reformation* (Boston & Edinburgh, 1926).

Nashe, Thomas, *The Works of Thomas Nashe*, ed. R. B. McKerrow, 5 vols. (London, 1904-10).

Nestle, Wilhelm, "Die Fabel des Menenius Agrippa", *Klio*, XXI (1927), 350-60.

Owst, G. R., *Literature and Pulpit in Medieval England* (Cambridge, 1933).

Painter, William, *The Palace of Pleasure*, ed. Joseph Jacobs, 3 vols. (London, 1890).

Palmer, John, *Political Characters of Shakespeare* (London, 1948).

Parson, Wilfred, "The Medieval Theory of the Tyrant", *The Review of Politics*, IV (1942), 129-43.

Patrick, J. Max, "Robert Burton's Utopianism", *Philological Quarterly*, XXVII (1948), 345-58.

Patrologia Latina, ed. Jean-P. Migne, 222 vols. (Paris, 1844-65).

Pearl, ed. E. V. Gordon (Oxford, 1953).

Pettet, E. C. "*Coriolanus* and the Midlands Insurrection of 1607". *Shakespeare Survey*, III (1950), 34-42.

Phillips, James E., *The State in Shakespeare's Greek and Roman Plays* (= Columbia University Studies in English and Comparative Literature No. 149) (New York, 1940).

Philo Judaeus, *Philo*, trans. F. H. Colson, 10 vols (= *Loeb Library*) (Cambridge, Mass., & London, 1939-41).

Pinto, Vivian de S., *The English Renaissance: 1510-1688*, 2nd ed. (New York, 1950).

Plato, *Crito*, trans. Harold N. Fowler (= *Loeb Library*) (London & New York, 1928).

——, *The Laws*, trans. R. G. Bury, 2 vols. (= *Loeb Library*) (London & New York, 1924).

——, *The Republic*, trans. Paul Shorey, 2 vols. (= *Loeb Library*) (London & New York, 1930).

——, *Timaeus*, trans. R. G. Bury (= *Loeb Library*) (London & New York, 1929).

Plessow, Max, *Geschicht der Fabeldichtung in England bis zu John Gay*, Palaestra LII (Berlin, 1906, rpr. New York, 1967).

Plutarch, *The Lives of the Noble Grecians and Romanes*, trans. *Thomas North*, 8 vols. (Stratford-upon-Avon, 1927).

Pollard, A. F., *Henry VIII* (London, 1905).

Ponet, John, *A Short Treatise of politike power* (Strassburg, 1556).

The Pricke of Conscience, ed. Richard Morris (Berlin, 1863).

The Princely Pellican (N.p., 1649).

Quarles, Francis, *The Complete Works in Prose and Verse*, ed. Alexander B. Grosart, 3 vols. (= *Chertsey Worthies' Library*) (Edinburgh, 1880).

Rabelais, François, *The Complete Works of Doctor Francis Rabelais*, trans. Thomas Urquhart and Peter Motteux, 2 vols (London, n.d.).

Respublica, ed. Walter W. Greg, EETS, O. S. 226 (Oxford, 1952).

Ribner, Irving, "The Tragedy of *Coriolanus*", *English Studies*, XXXIV (1953), 1-9.

Roe, Frederick W., *The Social Philisophy of Carlyle and Ruskin* (New York, 1921).

Ross, Malcolm M., *Milton's Royalism* (Ithica, N.Y., 1943).

Russell, H. K., "Tudor and Stuart Dramatizations of the Doctrines of Natural and Moral Philosophy", *Studies in Philology*, XXXI (1934), 1-27.

Sabine, George H., *A History of Political Theory*, 2nd ed. (New York, 1950).

Saxl, Fritz, *Lectures*, 2 vols. (London, 1957).

Schenk, Wilhelm, *Reginald Pole, Cardinal of England* (London, 1950).

Schroeder, Kurt, *Platonismus in der Englischen Renaissance: vor und bei Thomas Eliot*, Palaestra LXXXIII (Berlin, 1920).

Secor, Philip B., "Richard Hooker and the Christian Commonwealth", unpublished dissertation, Duke University, 1959.

Selden, John, *John Selden and His Table-Talk*, ed. Robert Waters (New York, 1899).

Sen, Sailendra K., "What Happens in *Coriolanus*", *Shakespeare Quarterly*, IX (1958), 331-46.

Seneca, *Ad Lucilium Epistulae Morales*, trans. Richard M. Gummere, 3 vols. (= *Loeb Library*) (Cambridge, Mass., & London, 1917-43).

——, *Moral Essays*, trans. John W. Basore, 3 vols. (= *Loeb Library*) (London & New York, 1927-35).

Shakespeare, William, *The Complete Plays and Poems of William Shakespeare*, ed. William A. Neilson and Charles J. Hill (Cambridge, Mass., 1942).

Shaw, G. Bernard, *The Collected Writings of Bernard Shaw*, 30 vols. (New York, 1930).

Shute, John, *The First and Chief Groundes of Architecture*, ed. Lawrence Weaver (London, 1912).

Sidney, Philip, *The Complete Works of Sir Philip Sidney*, ed. Albert Feuillerat, 4 vols. (Cambridge, 1912-26).

Sirluck, Ernest, "Milton's Political Thought: The First Cycle", *Modern Philology*, LXI (1964), 209-24.

Skeel, Caroline A. J., "The Influence of the Writings of Sir John Fortescue", *Transactions of the Royal Historical Society*, 3rd ser. X (1916), 73-114.

Smith, Edward, O., "The Elizabethan Doctrine of the Prince as Reflected in the Sermons of the Episcopacy, 1559-1603", *Huntington Library Quarterly*, XXVIII (1964), 1-17.

Smith, H. Maynard, *Henry VIII and the Reformation* (London, 1948).

Sophocles, *Works*, trans. Richard C. Jebb (New York & Cambridge, 1940).

The Spectator, ed. G. Gregory Smith, 4 vols. Everyman's Library (London & New York, 1907).

Spelman, John, *Certain Considerations Upon the Duties both of Prince and People* (Oxford, 1642).

Spencer, Herbert, *The Principles of Sociology*, 3rd. ed. 3 vols. (New York, 1897).

Spencer, T. J. B., "Shakespeare and the Elizabethan Romans", *Shakespeare Survey*, X (1959), 27-38.

Spencer, Theodore, *Shakespeare and the Nature of Man*, 2nd ed. (Cambridge, Mass., 1949).

Spitzer, Leo, *Clasical and Christian Ideas of World Harmony*, ed. Anna G. Hatcher (Baltimore, 1963).

Spurgeon, Caroline F. E., *Shakespeare's Imagery* (Cambridge, 1935).

Southey, Robert, *Sir Thomas More*, 2 vols. (London, 1829).

Starkey, Thomas, *England in the Reign of King Henry the Eighth*, ed. J. M. Cowper, EETS, E. S. 12, 32 (London, 1871-78).

——, *Exhortation to Unitie and Obedience* (London) n.d.

Stirling, Brents, *The Populace in Shakespeare* (New York, 1949).

Strauss, Leo, *The Political Philosophy of Hobbes*, trans. Elsa M. Sinclair (Chicago, 1952).

Strype, John, *Ecclesiastical Memorials*, 7 vols. (London, 1816).

Styles, Philip, "The Commonwealth", *Shakespeare Survey*, XVII (1964), 103-19.

Sutcliffe, Matthew, *A Treatise of Ecclesiastical Discipline* (London, 1590).

Talbert, Ernest W., *The Problem of Order: Elizabethan Political Commonplaces and an Example of Shakespeare's Art* (Chapel Hill, N. C., 1962).

Tanner, J. R., ed. *Tudor Constitutional Documents: A. D. 1485-1603* (Cambridge, 1922).

Tawney, R. H., and Eileen Power, ed. *Tudor Economic Documents*, 3 vols. (London, 1924).

Thucydides, *History of the Peloponnesian War*, trans. C. Foster Smith, 4 vols. (= *Loeb Library*) (London & New York, 1919-23).

Tilley, Morris P., "The Comedy of *Lingua* and the *Faerie Queene*", *Modern Language Notes*, XLII (1927), 150-57.

Tillyard, E. M. W., *The Elizabethan World Picture* (New York, 1944).

——, *Milton* (London, 1930).

Tomkis, Thomas, *Albumazar*, ed. Hugh G. Dick (= *University of California Publications in English* No. 13) (Berkeley & Los Angeles, 1944).

——, *Lingua*, in *Dodsley's Old English Plays*, ed. W. Carew Hazlett, 4th ed. 15 vols. (London, 1874), IX 331-463.

Trinterud, Leonard J., "The Origins of Puritanism", *Church History*, XX (1951), 37-57.

Ullman, Walter, *The Growth of Papal Government in the Middle Ages*, 2nd ed. (London, 1962).

Vindiciae contra tyrannos, trans. William Walker (1689), ed. H. J. Laski (London, 1924).

Webb, Clement C. J., *John of Salisbury* (London, 1932).

Wendell, Barrett, *William Shakespeare* (New York, 1899).

White, Helen C., *Social Criticism in Popular Religious Literature of the Sixteenth Century* (New York, 1944).

Whitgift, John, *The Works of John Whitgift*, ed. John Ayre, 3 vols. Parker Society (Cambridge, 1853).

Whitman, Walt, *The Complete Poetry and Prose* (New York, 1948).

Wilks, Michael, *The Problem of Sovereignty in the Later Middle Ages* (Cambridge, 1963).

Wolfe, Don M., "Milton and Hobbes: A Contrast in Social Temper", *Studies in Philology*, XLI (1944), 410-26.

——, *Milton in the Puritan Revolution* (New York, 1941).

——, ed. *Leveller Manifestoes of the Puritan Revolution* (New York, 1944).

Woodhouse, A. S. P., ed. *Puritanism and Liberty*, 2nd ed. (Chicago, 1951).

Woodstock: A Moral History, ed. A. P. Rossiter (London, 1946).

Wright, Thomas, ed. *Political Poems and Songs*, 2 vols. (= *Rolls Series*) (London, 1859).

Xenophon, *Memorabilia*, trans. E. C. Marchant (= *Loeb Library*) (London & New York, 1923).

Zagorin, Perez, *A History of Political Thought in the English Revolution* (London, 1954).

Zeeveld, W. Gordon, "*Coriolanus* and Jacobean Politics", *Modern Language Review*, LVII (1962), 321-34.

——, *Foundations of Tudor Policy* (Cambridge, Mass., 1948).

INDEX

DE PROPRIETATIBUS LITTERARUM

edited by

C. H. VAN SCHOONEVELD

Series Maior

1. Marcus B. Hester, *The Meaning of Poetic Metaphor: An Analysis in the Light of Wittgenstein's Claim that Meaning is Use.* 1967. 229 pp.
   f 36.— / $ 10.00

2. Rodney Delasanta, *The Epic Voice.* 1967. 140 pp.   f 22.— / $ 5.75

3. Bennison Gray, *Style: The Problem and its Solution.* 1969. 117 pp.
   f 23.— / $ 6.50

5. Raimund Belgardt, *Romantische Poesie: Begriff und Bedeutung bei Friedrich Schlegel.* 1970. 257 pp.   f 45.— / $ 12.50

Series Minor

1. Trevor Eaton, *The Semantics of Literature.* 1966. 72 pp.
   f 10.— / $ 2.80

2. Walter A. Koch, *Recurrence and a Three-Modal Approach to Poetry.* 1966. 57 pp.   f 10.— / $ 2.80

3. Nancy Sullivan, *Perspective and the Poetic Process.* 1968. 56 pp.
   f 10.— / $ 2.80

4. Donald LoCicero, *Novellentheorie: The Practicality of the Theoretical.* 1970. 120 pp.   f 16.— / $ 4.50

Series Practica

1. Robert G. Cohn, *Mallarmé's Masterpiece: New Findings.* 1966. 114 pp.
   f 22.— / $ 5.75

2. Constance B. Hieatt, *The Realism of Dream Vision: The Poetic Exploitation of the Dream-Experience in Chaucer and His Contemporaries.* 1967. 112 pp.   f 16.— / $ 4.00

3. Joseph J. Mogan Jr., *Chaucer and the Theme of Mutability*. 1969. 190 pp. ƒ 26.— / $ 7.45

4. Peter Nusser, *Musils Romantheorie*. 1967. 114 pp. ƒ 18.— / $ 5.00

5. Marjorie Perloff, *Rhyme and Meaning in the Poetry of Yeats*. 1970. 249 pp. ƒ 48.— / $ 13.75

6. Marian H. Cusac, *Narrative Structure in the Novels of Sir Walter Scott*. 1969. 128 pp. ƒ 20.— / $ 5.75

8. Victor W. Wortley, *Tallement des Réaux: The Man through his Style*. 1969. 99 pp. ƒ 22.— / $ 6.30

9. Donald R. Swanson, *Three Conquerors: Character and Method in the Mature Works of George Meredith*. 1969. 148 pp. ƒ 22.— / $ 6.30

10. Irwin Gopnik, *A Theory of Style and Richardson's Clarissa*. 1970. 140 pp. ƒ 22.— / $ 6.10

12. Sylvia D. Feldman, *The Morality-Patterned Comedy of the Renaissance*. 1971. 165 pp. ƒ 18.— / $ 5.00

13. Giles Mitchell, *The Art Theme in Joyce Cary's First Trilogy*. 1971. 136 pp. ƒ 18.— / $ 5.00

14. Dean Ebner, *Autobiography in Seventeenth-Century England: Theology and the Self*. 1971. 168 pp. ƒ 22.— / $ 6.10

15. Donald L. Ball, *Samuel Richardson's Theory of Fiction*. 1971. 323 pp. ƒ 36.— / $ 10.00

17. Meredith B. Raymond, *Swinburne's Poetics: Theory and Practice*. 1971. 202 pp. ƒ 36.— / $ 10.00

20. Edgar B. Schick, *Metaphorical Organicism in Herder's Early Works: A Study of the Relation of Herder's Literary Idiom to His World-view*. 1971. 135 pp. ƒ 25.— / $ 6.95

22. James E. Magner Jr., *John Crowe Ransom: Critical Principles and Pre-occupations*. 1971. 134 pp. ƒ 18.— / $ 5.00

23. Elisabeth Th. M. van de Laar, *The Inner Structure of Wuthering Heights: A Study of an Imaginative Field*. 1969. 262 pp. ƒ 36.— / $ 10.00

24. Bernard L. Einbond, *Samuel Johnson's Allegory*. 1971. 104 pp. ƒ 18.— / $ 5.00

27. Richard Vernier, *'Poésie ininterrompue' et la poétique de Paul Eluard*. 1971. 180 pp. ƒ 25.— / $ 6.95

28. Hugh L. Hennedy, *Unity in Barsetshire*. 1971. 144 pp. ƒ 28.— / $ 7.80

35. Roman Jakobson and Lawrence G. Jones, *Shakespeare's Verbal Art in Th'Expence of Spirit*. 1970. 32 pp. ƒ 10.— / $ 2.90

MOUTON · PUBLISHERS · THE HAGUE